Healthy Parenting

Other Books by Rick Johnson

That's My Son

Better Dads, Stronger Sons

The Power of a Man

Becoming Your Spouse's Better Half

That's My Teenage Son

That's My Girl

The Marriage of Your Dreams

How to Talk So Your Husband Will Listen

A Man in the Making

Romancing Your Better Half

10 Things Great Dads Do

Healthy Parenting

BECOME THE PARENT
YOU WISH YOU'D HAD

RICK JOHNSON

SPIRE

Published by Revell
a division of Baker Publishing Group
PO Box 6287, Grand Rapids, MI 49516-6287
www.revellbooks.com

Spire edition published 2020
ISBN 978-0-8007-3755-9

Previously published under the title *Overcoming Toxic Parenting*

Printed in the United States of America

Portions of several sections incorporate material from Rick Johnson's previous
books.

The author is represented by WordServe Literary Group.

20   21   22   23   24   25   26   7   6   5   4   3   2   1

To Karen—for all you deserved and didn't get,
and for all you got and didn't deserve,
you still have an awesome life ahead of you!
Be brave—you are more than you think possible.
I'm so proud of you.
I love you.

Contents

An unpredictable parent is a fearsome god in the eyes of a child.

—Susan Forward, *Toxic Parents*

The things they do to you . . . change you. Twist you. . . . We don't become the people we're supposed to be. We become . . . something else. . . . I wanted so much to be that girl. I was supposed to be, you know. They ruined me. They had no right, Danny. They had no right.

—Andrew Klavan, *A Killer in the Wind*

A Bad Childhood is easy to come by, and you don't have any control over that. A Good Life after a Bad Childhood is not easy to create, but you do have control over that. In a Bad Childhood you struggle against forces external to yourself. To come to a Good Life, the struggle is against forces internal—they *are* yourself.

—Dr. Laura Schlessinger,
Bad Childhood—Good Life

The greater the power, the more dangerous the abuse.

—Edmund Burke

Foreword

We were all raised in dysfunctional families. Some were more healthy than others, and some were more destructive than others, but because we are all sinners, all were dysfunctional. The more unhealthy a family, the more damage done to the children. And that damage affects our adulthood.

But like most people, we assume that how we were raised is similar to how others were raised—it was our normal. It may have included verbal abuse, physical abuse, sexual abuse, and/or isolation and neglectful abuse. But it was abuse in spite of how we may rationalize it. If what we had experienced were happening in a family next door to us, we wouldn't hesitate to call it abuse.

As a psychologist, counselor, and radio host, I talk often to deeply wounded people every day. Their lives have been devastated by the abuse they endured while growing up. Sometimes as we listen, it's so clear to us that the problem is a direct result of their childhood experiences. One question is all it takes to make the connection for them. So often it is like they had never before made the connection between what they struggle with today and their childhood experiences of yesterday. Instead of only operating in the past, those sins done to them are still in operation in their lives today.

In *Healthy Parenting: Become the Parent You Wish You'd Had*, Rick Johnson has written an extremely important book designed to help the average person recognize, understand, and then take steps to heal from their childhood wounds. He then takes the reader from an understanding of the importance of education, professional counseling, mentoring, and forgiveness to a strategic process that leads to healing and a newfound strength and empowerment.

I met Rick last year when we were on the same program at a large marriage conference. After listening to him, and seeing the response of the audience, I can tell you he speaks from experience. And what he says makes practical sense.

You are holding this book because you know it's time you put your past into the past so you can start living a life of joy, calm contentment, and eager optimism. And most of all, so that you can break the generational patterns that could so easily lead to a repetition of your childhood experiences with your own children. My prayer is that the accounts of other families and the principles in this book will begin the healing process for you and your family so you can be the transformation person in your generational patterns. Your kids are depending on you!

David Stoop, PhD
author of *Forgiving the Unforgivable*

Introduction

Pretty much everyone on the planet wants to be a good and loving parent. And unless we were blessed to be raised by really good parents, we want to be better parents than the ones who raised us. But for those raised by wounded, broken, or even downright evil parents, the challenge is how not only to break the habits that were modeled by those parents, but to figure out a healthy model to use in their place. That's a significant challenge, because we don't know what we don't know. It's not enough to say we don't want to do what our parents did—we have to have a positive model to fill that void or we fall back on what we know. In times of stress or pressure, we fall into old habits, emulating what was modeled for us as children by our permanent caregivers. This results in pain, guilt, and shame in both parents and children, causing those generational cycles and wounds to be passed on to a new generation.

Rather than repeat what was modeled by our parents for us as children, wouldn't it be nice to understand how to "turn the tables" and learn to become the kind of parents we long to be and wish we'd had?

Anyone who has come from a dysfunctional home life knows how difficult it is to begin to know how to be a healthy parent. For people who were abused or abandoned, those wounds compound our inability to parent our own children properly, especially if we do not understand and recognize what is motivating the decisions we make. Even if we weren't abused, many of us were fatherless or motherless, growing up as virtual orphans. No guidance is sometimes worse than bad guidance. Either way, this tends to perpetuate negative cycles or tendencies from generation to generation. For instance, our ministry works with many men in prison. Many of these men tell me their grandfathers and fathers were also in prison. They didn't intend to end up in prison, but it was the legacy they were given. We also work with lots of single moms and their children. Many of these moms tell me their grandmothers were single moms, their mothers were single moms, they were single mothers, and now their daughters are single moms. Truly they never wanted to be single moms, but that was what was modeled for them. Hence they tended to make decisions and choices (some even unconsciously) that led to them becoming single mothers. They then pass that programming on to their children.

The frustration of most parents in these circumstances is, *How do I learn to reprogram my thought process so I can make healthier choices?* Those snap decisions we make while under the stress and pressure of everyday life can make all the difference in what kinds of parents we become. Breaking those generational cycles requires both education and mentoring.

This book can be a significant resource in providing the educational part of that equation.

I was raised by a violent alcoholic mother and a narcissistic, codependent, alcoholic stepfather. In hindsight, many sick things occurred in our home, although they seemed normal at the time. Some of these things were nowhere near as severe as traumas other people had to endure, and some were much worse. And certainly many actions that are considered abusive today were normal behaviors in the 1960s. But the severity of our individual abuse is never the issue. Abuse of any kind is abuse—and it damages us. Some of the traumas my siblings and I endured included being slapped in the face repeatedly by my mother; receiving belt spankings on bare bottoms that left welts and sometimes drew blood (for an angry stepfather, where the belt hit was seldom a consideration); being screamed at in public; feeling verbally demeaned by being criticized, humiliated, and disgraced; being forced to sit at the dinner table for hours until we ate everything on our plate; witnessing multiple domestic violence incidents and the humiliating aftermath of police and ambulances coming to our home in the middle of the night; and enduring my mother's multiple suicide attempts and their fallout. But even more painful were the words used as weapons to wound a child's heart. That pain has lasted a lot longer.

My wife and I both come from very dysfunctional and abusive backgrounds. This has required us to engage in many years of individual and couples counseling. These experiences, as well as a wide variety of individual research and study on the topic of personal wounds (both personally and for the books I've written), have given me a strong background and passion for the subject matter. Healing my own childhood wounds and walking alongside my wife as she dealt with hers has given me unique insight into how those wounds affect our lives and the choices we make. In addition, the challenge of breaking the generational cycles associated with these dysfunctions has been an enlightening experience.

I share some of the experiences from my childhood in this book. Both of the parents who raised me have passed away. Anything I describe in this book is not meant to dishonor them or somehow exact revenge upon them by making them look bad. It is merely to help others who may have been through similar circumstances understand that they are not alone, and that there is hope.

Do you want to heal from childhood abuse and make a better life for you and your children? The actions I describe in this book take courage and persistence. They are not for the fainthearted. But I know from personal experience that they work. I believe they will work for you too. So, step up and hang on—you (and God) are about to change yourself, and that will change the world around you! Try to relax—it'll be worth it.

1

When Parents Fail

Violent homes have the same effect on children's brains as combat on soldiers.

—Daniel Amen, MD

A significant number of people in our country are suffering the effects of being raised by emotionally destructive people. The Centers for Disease Control and Prevention and Kaiser Permanente's Health Appraisal Clinic in San Diego collaborated on a study. They surveyed 17,000 Kaiser members on whether they had experienced any of eight adverse childhood experiences (ACEs). These included:

emotional abuse
physical abuse
sexual abuse

battered mother

parental separation or divorce

substance-abusing mother

mentally ill mother

incarcerated household member

Almost two-thirds of the participants reported at least one ACE, and more than one in five reported three or more.[1]

Being exposed to these kinds of experiences sets up patterns that influence or even control our daily lives as adults. Those patterns are then modeled for our own children and eventually get passed down to the next generation. Behaviors such as addictions, abusive actions, alcoholism, and abandonment get passed down from one generation to the next, often resulting in ongoing generational cycles. And when we feel bad about ourselves (like wounded people do), we tend to take it out on other people (like our spouse and children), usually those who cannot defend themselves.

Of course, not everyone who comes from an abusive home abuses their children. Some people are successful at breaking those cycles. We have a tendency to believe that all abusers were abused themselves. That's not entirely true. Only about 40 percent of parents who suffered from abuse go on to abuse their own children.[2] Yet, any number of abused children is too many.

Parents play a huge role in a child's feelings about themselves—for good or bad. Susan Forward, PhD, in her book *Toxic Parents: Overcoming Their Hurtful Legacy*, says, "Our parents plant mental and emotional seeds in us—seeds that grow as we do. In some families, these are seeds of love, respect, and independence. But in many others, they are seeds of fear, obligation, or guilt."[3]

If you are reading this book, you or someone you love may have been abused or raised in an abusive environment. Let's take a moment to learn about what abuse is, what it looks like, and how it affects us as adults and parents. Then once we've educated ourselves on what we are up against, we can move forward to the good news—change is possible!

Let's begin by looking at how an abusive family functions.

The Family System of Abuse

Our family constitutes our entire reality as a child. It teaches us who we are and how we are supposed to interact with the world. Good families give us the skills and encouragement to interact successfully with the world and other people. They teach us to lead a successful life. Toxic families teach us survival skills that may or may not translate into leading a successful life. Because of this, many abused people make self-defeating choices like believing they can't trust anybody, that they aren't worthy of being loved, or that they will never amount to anything. They are programmed to conform to the dysfunctional behaviors of the family. People from abusive families are taught that to be different is bad—they must conform and obey the rules of the family at all costs. To be different is to be a traitor—and being a traitor or turning on the family is high treason in abusive families.

Many families take on role-playing to perpetuate the family system. For instance, if Dad's role was to drink, Mom's role was to be codependent, and the children's roles were then

How Toxic Parents Cope

Toxic parents react to threats to their balance by acting out their fears and frustrations, with little thought for the consequences to their children. Here are some common coping mechanisms:

- **Denial**—Denial that anything is wrong or that it will ever happen again. Relabeling is also denial—an alcoholic becomes a "social drinker."
- **Projection**—Abusive parents frequently accuse their children of the very inadequacies they suffer from.
- **Sabotage**—In dysfunctional homes, other family members assume the roles of rescuers and caretakers. If any family member begins to change or get healthy, it threatens the balance of the home, and the other members may unconsciously sabotage their chances of success so that things get back to normal.
- **Triangling**—One toxic parent may enlist a child as a confidant or ally against the other parent. The child is pressured to choose sides and becomes an emotional dumping ground for their parent's discomfort.
- **Keeping Secrets**—This turns families into private clubs. Children who hide abuse by saying she "fell down the stairs" are protecting the club from outside interference.[4]

to be the parents in the home. Children from dysfunctional homes often take on specific roles in the family.

Here are some common roles (my three siblings and I fit into these roles pretty clearly):[5]

The Rebel gets into trouble and is known as the "bad boy" or "bad girl." Their behavior often warrants attention, distracting everyone from the real issues at home. They are also known as the "scapegoat." They are ashamed of their family life and often the first to get into "recovery."

The Mascot/Clown uses comedy to ease tension and calm explosive situations. The humor helps a family in pain but is a temporary balm. This child is kind and good-hearted but never seems to grow up.

The Good Girl (or *Boy*) or *Golden Child* is dutiful and respectable. They get good grades, don't make waves, and are often a confidant of a parent. They are fixers of the family but never get their needs met. They can be rigid, judgmental, and controlling. They are very self-sufficient and usually very successful in life but lack emotional intimacy.

The Lost Child becomes invisible. They stay out of the house by escaping into activities, friendships, or sports. They escape from reality but are generally very sad and angry, which they deny and avoid.

Parents are godlike in their positions in the home. They provide sustenance and shelter, make rules, and dole out pain, whether it's justified or not. Without parents, children instinctively know they would be unprotected, unfed, and unhoused. They would be in a constant state of terror, unable to survive alone.[6]

Abusive homes tend to have common characteristics, including the appearance of normalcy, emotional isolation, secrecy, neediness, stress, and lack of respect.

All children have certain rights. They have the right to have basic needs met, such as being fed, clothed, sheltered, and protected. They also have the right to be nurtured emotionally, the right to make mistakes, and the right to be disciplined without being physically or emotionally abused. Unfortunately, these rights are seldom honored in abusive homes.

However, most people (especially abused ones who crave parental nurturing) still have a need to deify their parents—no matter how bad they were. Many victimized people still believe their parents' behavior was justified: "I guess I probably deserved it" or "Sure I was beaten, but I turned out okay." Abusive parents have a propensity to deny that any abuse happened or they justify it. Just because inadequate parents "didn't mean it" doesn't mean it didn't hurt and cause harm. Intentionality is not a prerequisite of abuse. We hear people excuse these parents by saying things like "they didn't mean to do any harm" or "they did the best they could." Too often inadequate parents expect their children to somehow take care of *them* and meet *their* needs—tasks children are not capable of fulfilling. I truly didn't believe that many of the behaviors my parents exhibited were abusive until enough counselors and friends pointed it out or asked if I would ever treat my children that way.

Since many of us either deny we were abused or justify our parents' behavior, let's look at some specific types of abuse. It's hard to break a behavior (and heal a wound) if we are not aware of it or refuse to acknowledge it.

Abandonment

Not receiving the necessary psychological or physical protection a child deserves equates to abandonment. Being abandoned tells a child, "You are not important—you are not of value." Abandoned children then develop a deep sense of toxic shame. They grow up to believe that the world is unsafe, people cannot be trusted, and they do not deserve love and care. Abandoned children often believe that they cannot live up to their parents' expectations (which are often unrealistic), that they are held responsible for other people's behavior, and that their parents' disapproval is of the child's personhood rather than their actions. Common beliefs include:

- It's not okay to make a mistake.
- It's not okay to show your feelings.
- It's not okay to have needs—everyone else's needs are more important.
- It's not okay to have successes—accomplishments are not acknowledged or are discounted.[7]

My wife, Suzanne, was abandoned by both her father (whom she only met briefly twice) and by her mother, who quit parenting her at ten years old (Suzanne subsequently left home at age thirteen). Hence she had great abandonment issues when we got married. She didn't trust that I wouldn't abandon her, and she jealously guarded her heart. Being abandoned again was her greatest fear. She even had a tendency to try to push me to the point where I would leave (probably an unconscious attempt to test my level of commitment). It has taken the better part of three decades of modeling commitment on my part for her to start trusting that I will not abandon her. My level of commitment has at best healed and at worst scarred over the jagged wound of abandonment in her heart.

Our ministry works with hundreds of boys and girls (and adults) who have been abandoned by their fathers. To a person, they struggle with issues like self-esteem, self-confidence, risk taking, trying new things, fear of failure, and developing intimate relationships.

These problems manifest themselves in several ways. Many girls, who so ache for a father's love, willingly accede to the sexual advances of the predatory (and equally father-less) boys who eagerly take their love before tossing them aside like used tissues. One of the effects of being father-less is boys trying to feel like men or cross the threshold of manhood through sexual conquest of girls. The effects of fatherlessness on girls is just as damaging, resulting in the longing and desperate search for affection through sexual encounters with boys. What a damaging collision of the effects of fatherlessness.

One woman said this about her childhood: "I think the biggest wound is abandonment from a father. Mine left when I was fourteen. This was especially devastating because our home was really a 'happy one.' We all got along, and there were no signs of problems. But then, midlife crisis hit my father. And he was gone. Everything fell apart."

For this woman, abandonment has plagued her entire life: "Abandonment has been the greatest issue for me. Divorce and abuse plagued my life. Believing I am worthy and capable of a peaceful life has been a challenge. My core unhealthy belief I came to believe from my brokenness . . . I will never measure up to others' expectations, therefore I'm not worthy of love."

We even see children adopted into loving homes who still struggle with abandonment issues well into adulthood. Kids who are abandoned develop attachment disorders and fear close relationships. Sometimes even with God. If an earthly father (or mother) does not love you enough to stay, how devastating would it be for a heavenly Father to abandon you as well?

Emotional or Psychological Abuse

Emotional abuse impairs a child's emotional development and sense of self-worth. This type of behavior might include screaming, name-calling, criticism, sarcasm, belittling, humiliating, threats, rejection, or withholding love and support. It is frequently present in combination with other forms of abuse.

Some professionals think that emotional or psychological abuse is even more devastating than physical abuse. This is because the wounds on the outside heal much sooner than the wounds on the inside.

When we are wounded (especially in childhood), we tend to create "self-talk" related to that wound. For instance, if you've been abused, you might feel unworthy or that you somehow deserved to be abused. Additionally, words spoken to us by our care-providers tend to embed themselves in our hearts. If a father or mother tells us we are "no good" or "stupid," we tend to subconsciously believe that. Our unconscious mind then creates "tapes" that play those words over and over again, even when we don't recognize it is happening. This phenomenon causes us to self-sabotage throughout life as those old tapes roll over and over again, telling us what we cannot accomplish and why. However, those tapes are almost never true. We all have that little voice in our head that speaks to us. Often that voice repeats things we've heard our parents say about us. Abused children have voices that speak lies to them: "You're worthless," "You'll never amount to anything," or even "I wish you'd never been born." Those voices are madness to our souls and create great hopelessness.

Even when we are grown, our parents can exert great psychological power over us. When I finally worked up the courage to share my newfound Christian faith with my mother, she responded back with a letter saying, "You're just using religion as an excuse to get people to like you. If they knew you like I do, they'd hate you too." Even as an adult, those words stung deeply.

I always felt different than my parents—like I never belonged to them. I remember daydreaming as a child that I had been adopted and that this was all a big mistake. That someday I would find the good and loving people who were really my parents. Toxic parents tend to see their children's individual differences as a personal attack, and they defend themselves by fostering a child's helplessness and dependence. Because denial and the charade of normalcy are huge in abusive families, anyone who fights against those lies is subject to extra scorn and contempt. Because I refused to believe that the way my family lived was "normal," I was rejected and labeled a "bad" guy who thought he was better than everyone else. Writing this book has caused me to take a new look at my childhood. One thing I've discovered is how courageous I actually was as a young boy. To reject those stereotypes took great courage. But that rebellion earned me even more emotional abuse.

Verbal Abuse

Similar to emotional and psychological abuse is verbal abuse. Verbal abuse is often how emotional abusers deliver their wounds. There are two types of verbal abusers: the first are those who attack directly and openly, degrading their children. They call their children "stupid," "worthless," or "ugly." Even jokingly calling children derogatory terms such as "turd" or "chubby" is harmful and can do lasting damage. Insults like these from parents' mouths are like brands searing a child's soul. They might say things like they wish their child had never been born (perhaps the cruelest thing a parent can say to a child) and their constant assaults deeply wound their child's developing self-esteem. The second type of verbal abuser is more indirect, using a constant barrage of teasing, sarcasm, insulting nicknames, and subtle putdowns.[8]

And so even when children do succeed, a parent will deflate them, saying things like, "You're not so great," or "Who do you think you are," or "Anyone could have done that." And if children failed, you can be sure they would be told that they didn't have what it took anyway. Often these kids just give up and stop trying anything rather than be humiliated. Even when they do succeed at something, they tend to feel guilty and find ways to self-sabotage. The parent's negative words then become a self-fulfilling prophecy. Good parents use their words to lift up and empower their children. Bad parents use them to wound and control them.

Why do we care so much what our parents say or think of us? Parents are the center of a child's universe. If your all-knowing parents think bad things about you, they must be true—we have no other perspective to compare it against.[9] I remember the internal confusion this caused in my life as the things my parents said to me and believed about me were clearly not true compared to my experience. Of course later this confusion turned to anger when I finally figured out my parents were just liars.

And it doesn't seem to matter how old we get. Our parents still have the power to assault us verbally. When I signed a contract to write my first book, my brother told me the first thing my stepfather said when he found out was, "What in the world does Rick know about writing a book?" Pretty much the opposite response I would have if one of my children became a published author.

Adolescence can be an especially troubling time in an abusive home. Beyond all the normal problems exacerbated by puberty, girls blossoming into womanhood can be a threat to the beauty and sexuality of an older woman. They are seen as competition by Mom and are belittled whenever possible. Young males threaten a man's power and virility. The older male will use ridicule and humiliation to keep a boy feeling small and impotent. This behavior causes many teens to either act out in rebellion and defiance or shut down and be afraid to do anything for fear of being humiliated.

Words are powerful—they have meaning. They also have consequences. Research shows that shaming of a male child by his father is the single biggest contributor to that boy becoming a man who abuses women.[10] The old saying about "sticks and stones" is not true. Words do hurt. Sometimes for a lifetime.

Physical Abuse

Most of us have had an urge to hit our child from time to time—usually when they nag or defy us or won't stop crying. Thankfully the majority of parents are able to control those impulses. Often it has less to do with the child's behavior and more to do with our own levels of stress, exhaustion, and unhappiness. Author Susan Forward says, "Physical violence against children is often a reaction to stress at work, conflict with another family member or friend, or general tension over an unsatisfying life."[11]

Wounded people tend to lash out at those nearest to them—probably because they are easy targets due to their close proximity. Sandra Wilson, PhD, in her book *Hurt People Hurt People*, says this: "If I overpower, dominate, and abuse you today, it temporarily numbs the pain I still have because I was overpowered, dominated, and abused yesterday. Apparently victims gain a sense of inner strength and personal mastery by dominating someone even more powerless than themselves."[12]

For these parents, their children are merely a commodity to meet their own unmet needs.

> Many physically abusive parents enter adulthood with tremendous emotional deficits and unmet needs. Emotionally, they are still children. They often look upon their own children as surrogate parents, to fulfill the emotional needs that their real parents never fulfilled. The abuser becomes

Parents Who Physically Abuse Their Children Share Certain Characteristics

- They have an appalling lack of impulse control.
- They assault their children whenever they have strong negative feelings they need to discharge.
- They have little, if any, awareness of the consequences of what they are doing to their children.
- The abuse is almost an automatic reaction to stress—the impulse and the action are one and the same.[13]

enraged when his child can't meet his needs. He lashes out. At that moment, the child is more of a surrogate parent than ever, because it is the abuser's parent at whom the abuser is truly enraged.[14]

I think any rational, sane person knows you do not hit or strike a child. (Let's assume there is a difference between light physical punishment for discipline purposes and abusive behavior. I address this issue further in chap. 7.) But those who have been victimized by physical violence will find it very difficult to overcome and heal from this abuse without the help of a good counselor. The tragedy is, if we do not heal, we may inflict that same behavior on our own children.

Incest or Sexual Abuse

One of the oldest taboos in the civilized world may be that of incest. The Bible addresses this issue in 2 Samuel 13 with the story of Amnon and Tamar. Amnon was King David's firstborn son. Tamar was his younger sister for whom he lusted. Amnon devised a plan to fake illness in order to get the virgin Tamar to come to his residence to cook for him. He then lured her to his bedroom and raped her. Once finished, his lust turned to hatred. (This may be common in instances of incest, as it absolves the attacker of blame and places it on the victim. It also probably involves some transference of self-hatred as well.) He cast her out and shamed her. The passage says she "remained desolate in her brother Absalom's home" (NKJV). Interestingly, it says that when David found out what Amnon had done, he was angry, but it doesn't say that he took any action to provide justice for Tamar. That would have compounded the feelings of betrayal, injustice, and humiliation she must have felt. Several years later, Absalom murdered Amnon for his transgressions.

Approximately 90 percent of sexually abused children know their abuser. Incest is the cruelest betrayal of trust between a child and parent and understandably has emotionally devastating consequences. When an older sibling or relative is involved, it's just as damaging. Being sexually violated as a child is one of the worst evils most people will ever experience. When someone who is supposed to protect you ends up violating you, it is thoroughly destructive. Statistically one in three girls and one in six boys will suffer unwanted sexual experiences before the age of eighteen. That number is probably higher, as it is estimated that a high number of people never tell anyone they have been molested. Regardless, those conservative estimates alone translate into about 60 million people in our country having been victims of sexual abuse. Literally, everywhere you go, you will be in contact with someone who has suffered this fate. Look around you. In a room full of women, at least a third of them have been sexually abused as a child. This *has* to stop. If this is your legacy, you can stop it in your lineage by following some of the steps detailed throughout this book.

It's estimated that up to 90 percent of all incest victims never tell anyone. Why? Because they are afraid of breaking up the family. "Incest may be frightening, but the thought of being responsible for the destruction of the family is even worse."[15]

And the damage is even worse if the victim experiences any pleasure from these acts, as their shame is magnified. Our bodies are designed to be sexual beings. In addition, they are biologically programmed to respond (often as a form of physical protection) to sexual acts even in cases of non-consent and assault. This causes many victims to feel responsible for the event. Understand, as a child you were always the victim, whether you derived pleasure or not. The adult is *always* the one to blame in those circumstances.

Additionally, people do not tell anyone because incest abusers are very adept at psychological manipulation and fearmongering. They use threats and manipulation to keep their victims quiet.

Survivors of incest often report feeling worthless, bad, dirty, and damaged. Depression is a common result of incest. Women especially may allow themselves to become overweight as adults. This serves two purposes: (a) she imagines it will keep men away from her, and (b) the body mass creates the illusion of power and strength. Like many victims of abuse, incest survivors frequently self-medicate their pain with drugs and alcohol.[16]

Threats Used by Incest Abusers

Tell and I'll kill you.
Tell and I'll kill your parents/siblings/grandparents.
Tell and no one will believe you.
Tell and your mommy will be mad at (or hate) you.
Tell and people will think you are crazy.
Tell and I'll go to jail and there won't be anyone to support the family.[17]

Men who have been sexually abused have a special set of challenges to deal with, as it strikes at the heart of their masculinity. Men are not supposed to be assaulted, vulnerable, dominated, raped, or controlled. They may feel emasculated or that they are destined to be a homosexual.

Men generally find themselves uncomfortable dealing with and expressing emotions. In part, it's how they're brought up. Any form of sexual abuse creates intense emotions. Here are some common emotions men feel in these situations:

- *Dehumanized*—They feel like they have no value and constantly compare themselves to other men.

- *Shame*—They transfer false shame and guilt to themselves.

- *Ambivalent*—They can understand the emotion of anger, but not love. During the abuse they were feeling horrified and scared but also aroused. Their mind was saying, "This is not right," but their body is designed to respond when stimulated.

- *Impotent*—A word no man even wants to think about. They believe they have no voice—that no one will listen to them.
- *Disrespected*—They don't feel other men will respect them. That they will make fun of them. That they never measure up. Often they will become very promiscuous in an attempt to prove their masculinity (to themselves and the world).

We will talk more about protecting your children from incest or sexual abuse in chapter 8. In the meantime, please understand that incest affects us in very subtle and damaging ways. This is another type of abuse that may require very intense counseling in order to heal from. Don't wait! The longer you put it off, the more difficult it becomes.

Neglect

Neglect is the failure of a parent to provide for a child's basic needs. Neglect can take place in many forms and is the most common type of abuse in which authorities get involved. Starvation and malnutrition, unsanitary conditions, dangerous living environments, and lack of nurturance and supervision are all part of neglecting the needs of a child. Drug addicts commonly have children removed from their home for neglecting them in one way or another.

One particularly insidious form of neglect is Munchausen syndrome by proxy (also known as Factitious Disorder Imposed on Another). It is a form of child abuse where the caretaker (usually the mother) either "makes up fake symptoms or causes real symptoms to make it look like the child is sick."[18] Tactics used may include withholding food so it appears the child can't gain weight, giving the child drugs or chemicals to cause vomiting or diarrhea, infecting IV lines to cause sickness, or heating up thermometers to fake a fever in the child. These mothers often work or have worked in the health care industry and know a lot about medical care. They appear devoted to their child and are highly involved with the health care team, describing their child's symptoms in great detail. The child's symptoms are often reported by the mother but disappear by the time the child is hospitalized, reappearing when the child goes home. Because of this, the health care professionals often think she is a great mother because of her dedication to her sick child. The child is often taken to a wide range of doctors and hospitals in order to hide the pattern of abuse. Munchausen cases are often fatal for the child.[19]

Neglect is not just failing to meet the basic survival needs of a child. It can include lack of nurturing as well. A syndrome first identified in a Romanian orphanage during the communist era, *failure to thrive* (FTT) is the term given to the babies who had their basic needs for food and shelter met but were never held or nurtured. The babies began dying because of lack of human touch and nurturance. Later in life, many of the orphans who did survive suffer from maladies such as attention deficit hyperactivity disorder (ADHD), post-traumatic stress disorder (PTSD), bipolar disorder, attachment disorder, and other psychiatric illnesses.[20]

Neglect can also consist of a parent who doesn't love their child, is contemptuous of them, is emotionally uninvolved, or just ignores them. It is a cruel form of child abuse.

Alcoholism

> Growing up in the chaos and unpredictability created by alcoholism caused many of us to mask our confusion, anger, and shame by trying to be perfect. To prove to ourselves and the world that there was nothing wrong with us or our families, we scrambled hard in school to get straight A's, or worked feverishly at home to keep everything neat and tidy. We became star athletes, artists, corporation leaders, humanitarians, and outstanding citizens. Inside, however, we feel driven, terrified of failure, unable to relax or play, and lonely.
>
> —Al-Anon, *From Survival to Recovery*

One of my earliest memories is lying in bed at night under the covers, with my little brother and sisters huddled around me, while in my mind I begged God to make the hitting and screaming stop in the next room. This was a fairly frequent occurrence in our home while I was growing up.

Children of alcoholics soon discover they are more of an irritant than a blessing to their parents. That's just the tip of the iceberg of the legacy bestowed upon them. As author Susan Forward says, "Adult children of alcoholics have been handed a legacy of rage, depression, loss of joy, suspiciousness, damaged relationships, and overdeveloped sense of responsibility."[21]

The constant chaos of an alcoholic home often leads to controlling behavior and perfectionism in adult children of alcoholics in an effort to have some semblance of control and peace in their lives. As a recovering perfectionist, I still struggle with control issues. Being a perfectionist means you don't like surprises or even spontaneity very much. That takes away a lot of the joy in life.

Denial is huge in alcoholic families. It is the elephant in the room—always there taking up space and damaging things, but everyone conspicuously ignores it. In the home of alcoholics, you can't trust anyone or anything you see or experience. One day something you say or do is okay, even encouraged. The next day you get hit or shamed for the same thing. You always feel unbalanced, like you are on a ship in heavy seas. Everything is always *your* fault. That makes children of alcoholics need to always be in control in an attempt to keep the chaos in check.

Other forms of denial are foisted on children by enabling adults who say things like, "How dare you call your mother/father a drunk!" Shaming tactics include statements like, "Who do you think you are?" or "What makes you think you are better than we are?" You soon learn to live "down" to the expectations of your family. Or if you choose to be different you run the risk of being labeled as "bad" and are subject to much criticism and abuse. My role in my family was the "bad guy." Because I was embarrassed by their behavior and refused to worship it, my parents heaped scorn and blame upon me every chance they could.

My mother's behavior ranged from cloyingly loving to excruciatingly cruel, depending upon her mood and the amount of alcohol she had consumed. I constantly tried to second-guess how to get her approval or at least stay on her good side. Unfortunately, it was a no-win endeavor, as the floor kept shifting—the same behavior that pleased her one day would set her off into a rage the next. People from alcoholic homes quickly become afraid to try new things

The Three Elements of the Big Secret of Alcoholism

- The alcoholic's denial of his or her alcoholism in the face of overwhelming evidence to the contrary and in the face of behavior that is both terrifying and humiliating to other family members.
- The denial of the problem by the alcoholic's partner and frequently by other members of the family. They commonly excuse the drinker with explanations such as, "Mom just drinks to relax," "Dad tripped on the carpet," or "Dad lost his job because he has a mean boss."
- The charade of the "normal family," a façade that the family presents to one another and to the world.[22]

or take risks, which are behaviors required to be successful in life. Even when you succeed, an alcoholic parent will deflate you, saying things like, "You're not so great," or "It's about time you did something right," or "Anyone could have done that."

"'The charade of the normal family' is especially damaging to a child as it forces him to deny the validity of his own feelings and perceptions. It is virtually impossible for a child to develop a sense of healthy self-confidence if he has to constantly lie about what he is thinking and feeling."[23] It takes a tremendous amount of energy to keep the charade going, as the child must constantly be on guard, living in constant fear of accidently "spilling the beans" and betraying the family.[24] I remember as an adolescent being exhausted all the time but never knowing why. Now I understand.

The worst thing you can do in an alcoholic family is to tell outsiders that someone is an alcoholic inside the home. When I wrote my first book, *That's My Son*, I briefly mentioned that I was raised in an alcoholic home. I didn't name names or go into any further detail, just mentioned it in passing. My mother read the book (or at least that sentence) and was outraged. How dare I tell the world a lie like that! She didn't speak to me again for the next ten years until she became sick at the end of her life and needed me.

Mental Illness

About one of every twenty-five individuals in the United States is a sociopath, meaning they do not have a conscience.[25] My siblings believe that my stepfather was conscienceless. Judging by many of his actions, that may have been true.

My mother was probably a victim of incest during her childhood. She never addressed the wounds left by that experience. Although never diagnosed, it's my belief that she may have suffered from all or some combination of the following mental issues: bipolar disorder, borderline personality disorder, severe chronic depression, anxiety disorder, and post-traumatic stress disorder (PTSD). Toward the end of her life in hospice, she was put on antidepressants and was suddenly a completely different person. She was calm and rational, and her sense of humor stopped being biting and sarcastic. She was almost fun to be around. What kind of life could she have led had she sought help instead of self-medicating her entire life? What kind of children could she have raised had she been healthy and liked herself? Those are questions that will never be answered but that deserve consideration nevertheless.

It's completely reasonable to assume that if you experienced trauma or abuse as a child, you too suffer from PTSD. It's important that we understand what this is, what it looks like, and what it does, as it affects not only us but the people who love us as well. PTSD impacts not only military combat veterans but also anyone who has suffered physical, sexual, or emotional abuse as a child; rape; domestic violence; abortion; the traumatic death of a loved one (murder, suicide, etc.); or even having lived with someone who has PTSD. Symptoms of PTSD include flashbacks, nightmares, isolation, emotional numbing, depression, rage and anger, severe anxiety, guilt, denial, and thoughts of suicide. Characteristics of people who suffer from PTSD include workaholism, over-commitment, eating disorders, compulsive habits, impaired childhood memories, perfectionism, or martyr syndrome.[26]

One of the symptoms of PTSD that was described to me years ago is hypervigilance. The counselor asked me if, in a theater-style environment, I always sat either in a seat on the aisle (usually toward the back of the room) or, if in a restaurant, with my back to the wall. Was I always aware of where the exits were located and what was going on around me? I had to answer yes to both questions, always. Clearly, from those symptoms and many others, I had suffered PTSD from the violence and abuse in my childhood. While I've gotten better and we now joke about my compulsion to sit on an end seat, I still feel uncomfortable sitting in the middle of the row.

Here's what happens in our body when we have PTSD. When a threat occurs our brain sends a message to the adrenal glands, which produce two types of chemicals—adrenaline (which causes us to flee) or noradrenaline (which causes us to fight). Our bodies go into high gear and we respond by fleeing or fighting. A fight response would invoke behaviors like rage, anger, hyperactivity, impatience, or even abusive behavior. A flight response would exhibit frustration, isolation, low self-esteem/self-worth, depression, or suicidal thoughts. Here's the problem: the brain cannot differentiate between a real threat and an imagined one. So, that means if you've had a traumatic event in the past and something happens today that reminds you of that event (even things as simple as sounds or smells), it can trigger your brain to order the adrenal glands into action, even if there is no actual threat. The urge to fight or flee can be very strong, and if you don't know what is happening, you'll respond with irrational and inappropriate behaviors as the hormones flood your body.[27] One man told me that the odor of pomade in the hair of an older gentleman that he met triggered an almost irresistibly strong reaction to flee because it reminded him of his abuser. The smell of pomade makes him sick to his stomach to this day.

If you experience any of the symptoms described above, I encourage you to seek the advice of a mental health professional. PTSD is not something to mess around with or something you can control with your own willpower.

Now let's look at how past abuse affects us and our parenting.

2

How Our Past
Affects Our Own Parenting

Many of them have no idea why their lives aren't working.
Many more suffer from a damaged sense of self-worth because a parent had regularly hit them, or criticized them,
or "joked" about how stupid or ugly or unwanted they
were. Still others were overwhelmed with guilt, or sexually abused, or forced to take on too much responsibility.

—Susan Forward, PhD,
Toxic Parents

Why do some people from horrible backgrounds become
victims who live self-sabotaging lives and others from a
similar environment live healthy, happy, productive lives?
The answer to that question is "control." We all have free
will. We can make a decision to allow the past to control

us or we can control our lives despite the pain of our past. Quite literally, we can *decide* to live a good life or live one of misery.

I remember as a child making a promise to myself that I would never be like my parents. I would never live like them, I would never be an alcoholic, and I would have a "good" life. My wife came from a very violent background of mental and physical abuse, neglect, abandonment, and sexual abuse. In addition, her lineage was one of generational poverty and single motherhood. Statistically, she should be one of those people who repeat the generational cycles of divorce, chemical dependency, and promiscuity modeled for them during childhood. I asked her one day how she avoided those minefields and turned out to be such a healthy, happy, and loving person. She simply stated, "I made a decision not to live my life that way."

This means making a conscious decision not to focus on the past and the wounds that were inflicted upon you. It means looking forward instead of backward. It also means enjoying the good things we have today instead of letting the past ruin even those. Being thankful for what we have instead of what we missed out on. And finally it means doing what we need to do to heal from those wounds.

One thing we need to remember is this: We may have been powerless when bad things were done to us as a child. But we are not powerless as adults. In fact, we are more powerful now than our abusers. We are in control now. Of course if it were that easy, everyone would do it.

Let's see what the effects of a toxic childhood do to us so we can begin to understand how to overcome them and take control of our lives.

Programmed Outcomes

What does abuse during childhood do to our brains? First is the false shame and false guilt that we transfer upon ourselves. Why do we blame ourselves for the abuse instead of putting the accountability on the one who was responsible?

People raised by toxic parents suffer surprisingly similar symptoms: damaged self-esteem, leading to self-destructive behavior. Almost all feel worthless, unlovable, and inadequate. Consciously or unconsciously, almost all children blame themselves for their parent's abuse. "It is easier for a defenseless, dependent child to feel guilty for having done something 'bad' to deserve Daddy's rage than it is for that child to accept the frightening fact that Daddy, the protector, can't be trusted."[1] The only way abuse makes sense to a child is if they accept responsibility for the parent's behavior.[2]

Many people who have suffered from severe trauma also experience dissociation. Dissociation is similar to what is described as leaving your body. One online medical website defines it as "a perceived detachment of the mind from the emotional state or even from the body. Dissociation is characterized by a sense of the world as a dreamlike or unreal place and may be accompanied by poor memory of specific events."[3] This is suspected to be a coping or defense mechanism against something that is too traumatic or painful for the person to deal with.

Dissociation manifests itself in several ways:

- *depersonalization*—detached or out-of-body experience

- *derealization*—the sense that the world is not real, like watching life through a movie
- *dissociative amnesia*—inability to recall important personal information or events
- *identity confusion and identity alteration*—sense of confusion about who a person is or altering who they are[4]

Anxiety, PTSD, low self-esteem, somatization, depression, chronic pain, interpersonal dysfunction, and substance abuse, along with self-harm and suicidal actions are all potential manifestations people from toxic homes struggle with.

In chapter 1 we discussed a study done on people who had experienced ACEs (adverse childhood experiences). ACEs have a cumulative effect on humans with drastic results. For children who have experienced four or more ACEs, the outcomes include

- being 12 times more likely to attempt suicide
- being 10 times more likely to use drugs
- being 7 times more likely to abuse alcohol
- being 260 percent more likely to develop COPD (from smoking, etc.)
- having higher rates of heart disease, sexually transmitted diseases, and early death, which increase with the number of ACEs a person experiences[5]

The number of ACEs a person experiences as a child can determine the amount of medical care they will need as an adult with surprising accuracy. For instance, individuals with four or more ACEs were twice as likely to be diagnosed with cancer and 460 percent more likely to suffer from depression than those who had none. An ACE score of six or more short-ened a person's lifespan by nearly twenty years.[6]

Those are significant outcomes that we need to be aware of if we are to change our fate. *While those numbers may seem depressing, healing our internal traumas and wounds helps reduce those outcomes back down to within normal ranges.* Again, your past does not dictate your future.

Patterns

Children who have been abused internalize profoundly nega-tive messages about themselves and others. These messages persist into adulthood, impacting how they feel about them-selves. Perhaps most fundamentally, it hurts their ability to have intimate relationships. Abuse violates the trust at the core of a child's world, limiting their ability to have close rela-tionships and leading them into chaotic lifestyles. As a result of unresolved childhood abuse issues, many survivors' lives are typified by frequent crises, such as job disappointments, failed relationships, and financial setbacks. Possible reasons for this are that the internal chaos experienced by the person prevents them from being able to establish predictability, regularity, and consistency in their lives.

That said, it is possible to live a full and constructive life. And to even thrive—to enjoy a feeling of wholeness and sat-isfaction in your life, as well as genuine love and trust in your relationships. The first step toward recovery is to recognize the connection between your prior abuse and your current patterns of behavior.[7]

People who have been abused also tend to look at the world in black and white, with sort of an all-or-nothing thinking. This results in an "always" or "never" mentality that tends to be suspicious of others. For instance, an abused child might think, *Daddy abused me. Daddy is a man. Therefore men can't be trusted.* Or in a relationship, a wife might think, *He is mad at me. Therefore he does not love me.* They then carry that mentality throughout life in various circumstances even if they do so unconsciously.

People who have been abused tend to be people pleasers. They learned early on how to anticipate the abuser's emotional reactions. Pleasing the abuser was one way of reducing or limiting the amount of abuse. They often carry around a great deal of shame or guilt. This leads to high incidences of depression among this population. Survivors also tend to use coping strategies they learned in childhood, such as denying or minimizing the abuse they were exposed to.

Abuse also leads to addictions in its victims, with self-medications like drugs, food, gambling, or shopping. Other forms of abuse might include children who are born with fetal alcohol syndrome (FAS) or meth babies who have significant challenges to face in life. Finally, children who have been adopted or raised in foster care often face challenges such as attachment disorder, which makes it difficult to connect with others and control their emotions.

Modeled Behaviors

Have you ever wondered why people are attracted to the same chaos and destructive environments that they escaped from in childhood? You'll notice that if you put people who grew up in chaotic environments in peaceful situations, they will eventually create chaos. It's because they are uncomfortable in an environment that they are not used to. The brain, during times of stress and chaos, releases certain chemicals and hormones (cortisol, adrenaline, dopamine, and norepinephrine) to help the body cope and adapt to that environment. Soon, the body becomes accustomed to those high levels of chemicals. When the brain then finds itself in a peaceful situation, it slows production of those chemicals and the body experiences withdrawal-like symptoms, creating discomfort in the individual. A return to a chaotic environment raises the levels of chemicals again, and the body calms down—much like someone addicted to drugs. We all seek familiar patterns in life, even if they are painful or destructive. These familiar patterns create comfort and structure in our lives because it is what we are used to. Being in a familiar environment means we know the rules and what to expect.

And the more shamed we feel, the more likely we are to believe that painful love is better than no love at all. Why would a woman (or a man) continue to either return to an abusive spouse, or seek out other men who abuse her? It's because what we were raised with is familiar. We are more comfortable with that than the unfamiliar. Additionally, people who have been abused begin to believe they deserve to be treated that way. It's part of who they are—part of their identity. Given the choice, many wounded people do not believe they truly deserve to be treated in a loving, adoring manner.

Breaking Generational Cycles

Generational cycles are behaviors that are modeled for children to the point that they get passed down from one generation to the next (often for multiple generations). The younger generation grows up and emulates the behaviors that were modeled for them by the parents or important caregivers. When parents mislead their family, the repercussions are often felt for generations—the Bible says that the sins of the father will be passed down to the third and fourth generation (Exod. 20:5). Common generational cycles include behaviors such as alcoholism, drug addictions, abandonment, domestic violence, abuse, or divorce. When these types of behaviors are prevalent in family behavior, at least one or more of the children will usually grow up and engage in them as well. Some of this may be genetic (as we will see in chap. 7) but often it is a case of "monkey see, monkey do."

I work with many men who were abandoned by their fathers during childhood. Even though they firmly claim they will never abandon their children, they often end up in that circumstance anyway. I also see it in women whose mothers and grandmothers were single moms. Despite their best intentions, they often follow in the footsteps modeled for them. I also do a lot of work with men in prison. Many of them share with me that their fathers and grandfathers were in prison. They never intended to go to prison, but they were programmed to make choices that led them down that path. Sons who have fathers in prison are seven times more likely to end up incarcerated than boys whose dads were not imprisoned.

Generational cycles are difficult to change, but it is possible. People who did not have loving, caring parental behaviors modeled for them are not doomed to pass those behaviors on to their children. Just because we didn't (or still can't) get love and nurturing from our parents doesn't mean we can't give it to our kids. It's just difficult when our emotional accounts are low and being drained without replenishment.

Our pain and neediness cause us to act in ways that we don't like and often can't control. Breaking generational cycles requires us to do two things: (1) become educated on what is happening, and (2) find mentors in our lives who can model and teach us what healthy relationships look like. Being educated on the process taking place between childhood abuse, with the damage it creates in our minds and psyches, and the effects it creates in adulthood is the first step to healing those wounds. But education alone is generally not enough. You have to be guided (probably by professional help) to discover epiphanies and to learn coping mechanisms. You also need good, healthy people around you to show you and teach you what good marriages and parenting look like. It will require strong determination and intentionality—those who break generational cycles are to be commended, as it takes a lot of grit and willpower.

Here's another thing we need to remember. Sometimes we can get so caught up in trying to change, to do it "right," that we can forget the most important thing—to just love our kids. That's really what they need. Love covers a lot of mistakes. Just love them.

Disadvantages of Poverty

> Certain athletes who grew up in the Depression played that way, the mongrels of poverty tearing at their calves.
>
> —Roger Kahn, *The Boys of Summer*

Poverty can be a form of abuse. Certainly it structures the way we see the world and interact with it. If you have grown up in poverty, you can't change yourself on your own. Your environment and the emotional cues it sends, along with the unconscious cultural influences, overpower your conscious intent, causing you to make choices that keep you at the same socioeconomic level.

Children in poverty are at greater risk for a number of outcomes, including poor academic achievement, school dropout, abuse and neglect, physical health problems, and developmental delays. Psychosocial problems may include impulsiveness, difficulty getting along with peers, aggression, ADHD, and conduct disorder. They have higher rates of anxiety, depression, and low self-esteem. Physical health problems include low birth weight; poor nutrition; chronic conditions, such as asthma and pneumonia; risky behaviors, like smoking and early sexual activity; and exposure to violence. Parents in poverty experience chronic stress, depression, and marital distress, and exhibit harsher parenting behaviors.[8]

So if we were raised in poverty and want to change our socioeconomic status in order to keep our children away from its effects, what are some things we need to keep in mind? First of all, your family might despise you for trying to break out of poverty—for thinking you are "better" than they are. If you do succeed they will likely not be proud of you no matter how badly they turned out. In fact they will probably resent you on some level. Know that you may have to sever relationships with many of your existing friends and family. As difficult as that may be, the positive change for your future and your family's future is worth it.

Second, understand that some of the "hidden rules" of poverty must be broken in order to succeed in life. All socioeconomic classes have hidden rules that are known only to that class. You generally only discover those rules by someone in that class explaining them to you. Learning the rules of the class you want to move into is imperative in order to make the jump. For instance, in generational poverty children are considered possessions. Education is generally feared because when children get educated they leave, causing you to lose your possessions. Or you might be skeptical of education because you don't think it makes a difference in anyone's life—at least it didn't in yours anyway (even though education is one of the fundamental requirements to escape from poverty). Also, physical discipline is very acceptable in poverty.[9]

Different attitudes and belief systems are more prevalent in poverty than in other classes. These attitudes might result in actions such as coarse language or humor (inappropriate or off-color jokes), resentment of authority (telling your boss off for a perceived slight), using physical violence to solve problems (defending your wife's honor when it wasn't really questioned), or a short-sighted vision that encourages spending all your money to the exclusion of paying your bills (paid on Friday, broke by Monday). This causes lack of acceptance by the other social classes and generally keeps us from getting ahead in life.[10]

Of course how you dress, act, and carry yourself also tells a lot about your socioeconomic class. A story I related in a previous book illustrates my point:

> A woman came up to me after I had spoken at a conference and said, "I loved your talk and speaking style. You remind me of an educated workingman." I must admit I didn't really know whether that was a compliment or a criticism.

After reflection, I realized she had that impression because that's exactly what I am. I was raised in a lower middle class, blue-collar neighborhood. Both my parents were straight off the farm from Wisconsin. Despite the fact that I have a graduate degree I have a working-class pedigree.

That comment got me to thinking about how we are raised and how much we are actually able to change from our early childhood programming. For instance, I have well exceeded the socioeconomic status of my upbringing—I am college educated, have started several successful businesses, am a published author, and interface successfully with people from all walks of life. Yet something about me (within me) told that woman what my background was and—in essence—*who* I was. Our roots develop within us a character or personification that no matter how much we might try to change, our heritage remains. It shows in our mien, our demeanor, our attitude, how we carry ourselves, even how we talk and walk. It shows up in our language and communication style—our accents, our inflections, our emphasis on certain words and the colloquialisms we use. It shows in the clothes we wear, how we wear them, our style or élan, and our belief or attitude of where we belong in the world.

Psychologically it shows in how we feel about ourselves (our self-esteem) and how we see ourselves (our self-image). Despite the fact I have had years of counseling, training, education, and intentional growth, I still have some essence of blue-collar workingman in me.

You'll notice that people can always pick out those who are not from their background (it's pretty easy to tell the difference between someone raised in an affluent area of Boston versus someone from a poor neighborhood in Birmingham, Alabama). The poor kid who gets a scholarship to Harvard or Princeton is glaringly out of place and never quite fits in. Even the middle-class kid who goes to a poor neighborhood stands out like a sore thumb. Try as we might to bury it, our past hovers over us like the shadows in a graveyard. Oftentimes it doesn't matter how we dress or how much education we have. Even wearing an expensive suit and watch with Italian loafers, I probably would not be as comfortable in a big corporate boardroom environment as someone who grew up with that expectation and training. My demeanor, attitude, and language would give me away (although I've learned one way to make people think I'm smarter than I am is to just keep my mouth shut).

My wife comes from a hardscrabble home life as well. Even in a designer gown with diamond earrings she might have a difficult time fitting in at a highbrow social function because she does not know the language, the habits, the customs, and the nuances of social protocol of people from that pedigree nor the confidence that comes with it (although my wife is a lot classier than I am and might be able to pull it off). My point is, even though she is just as intelligent and elegant as women from that background, she'll probably never be confused for someone who has had debutante training and attended a finishing school before going off to Bryn Mawr, Radcliffe, or Vassar College.[11]

All that to say, you can jump economic classes with education and effort. My wife and I moved from poverty to middle class, and my relatives moved from middle class to wealth. America may be the only country on the planet where your past does not dictate your future. Make the jump. Your children will be served greatly and have big advantages by not being raised in poverty.

How Trauma Changes the Brain

Early childhood trauma changes the brain in a number of ways. These changes last a lifetime and can lead to adult depression, anxiety, substance abuse, and psychiatric disorders. Many trauma survivors are very resilient but struggle with these day-to-day issues. One way childhood abuse disrupts brain activity is by diminishing its capacity to handle stress. During times of stress, the body releases hormones such as cortisol. This release of cortisol is designed to be brief before it is shut down again. However, during times of severe abuse, the brain's ability to turn off that stress response is disabled. When that happens, cortisol remains in the brain, causing bad things to happen. High levels of cortisol cause mood changes, disturb sleep, heighten anxiety, and cause irritability. This leads to depression, PTSD, and other psychiatric disorders, which affect the victim's job performance and marriage and parenting relationships, and lead to higher instances of substance abuse.[12]

Frequently, then, victims with those kinds of issues run a higher-than-expected risk of becoming abusers themselves. Our childhood wounds cause reflexive responses in us as adults. We repeat ugly childhood dynamics in an attempt to repair deep childhood hurts and longings.[13] But take hope! As you're about to see in the following chapters, it is possible to heal and lead a healthy, happy, and productive life in spite of your past.

Sometimes people from abusive childhoods become career victims, becoming angry, bitter, self-destructive, or depressed. Author and radio host Dr. Laura Schlessinger says of people like this, "[They are] always unhappy, unbelievably demanding of others, a big chip on their shoulder, an even bigger attitude of entitlement, and generally a propensity for spreading ill cheer."[14]

Being a victim can give us an excuse for how our lives turn out. Victims are often rewarded for their bad behavior. Many times this happens because they surround themselves with people who will put up with them and cater to their desires. And frankly, no one expects much from people who suffer. It seems pretty cruel to expect accountability or responsibility from people who are emotionally bleeding all over themselves and others. Also, we learn early on in life that being sick can have its own rewards. Children with stomachaches get out of school, are exempt from chores, and get extra attention.

Don't be a professional victim. Yes, you got some bad breaks. But as you are about to see, things can get better. Your spouse and your children are depending on you.

3

Healing Our Wounds

The worst legacy one lives with from childhood abuse is
the ignorance on how to live a normal, balanced, healthy
adult life!

—Dr. Laura Schlessinger,
Bad Childhood—Good Life

Okay! Now that you have a better understanding of all the
bad stuff that happens to kids (and to you as well), let's spend
the rest of this book on positive, life-changing discussions.

I recently listened to a talk on the radio by neuropsy-
chologist Dr. Mario Martinez who said that all wounds can
be narrowed down to three categories: shame (which feels
hot in the body), abandonment (feels cold), and betrayal
(feels hot/anger). Shame, he said, is healed by experiencing
honoring. Abandonment is healed by experiencing commitment. And betrayal is healed by experiencing loyalty. If that's

true, understanding our wounds can tell us how to help heal those wounds or at least to more effectively deal with them.

In order to become the kind of parent you want to be, and the kind your children deserve, you have to first deal with your past issues. *Research shows that when a parent resolves their trauma issues, their children do well.* This is an ongoing, lifelong endeavor. It's a journey, not a destination. You'll never be completely "healed." But the good news is that it is never too late to begin, and it does get better—much better! Trust me on this.

This process includes healing from childhood wounds and learning what it means to be a healthy parent. Old childhood issues always surface during times of stress and pressure. I've known plenty of people who were pretty good at holding everything together until life's challenges snuck up on them and kicked the foundation out from under them. Having children is one surefire way for those old issues to raise their ugly head. This is because there is no way to avoid those issues once you have your own children. And if you haven't healed from your issues, you will start acting out in very strange ways, often emulating your parents. You will then begin feeling guilty, which exacerbates the problem even more. Throw in life's other stressful events, like marital issues, work problems, financial challenges, or the death of a loved one, and you suddenly find yourself overwhelmed without even knowing why.

Everyone has some wounds from childhood. Some are slight and barely noticeable; others are monsters that ravage a person's soul. I stated it this way on a chapter about woundedness in an earlier book:

The wounds that we receive to our heart and soul can either cripple us or motivate us to accomplish great things in life. Undoubtedly they are one of the biggest obstacles to having more intimacy in our relationship. Our wounds determine the way we respond to things that are said to us and how we treat others in our life. Wounds that are not dealt with sit and fester within us until they eventually spew their venom onto those we love and care about. But wounds that are healed can become a source of great inspiration and wisdom.[1]

If we don't heal a wound, it controls our life. This ensnares us and makes us vulnerable to toxic relationships and other unhealthy practices. Furthermore, our wound can become an idol that we worship. Some people hang on to their wounds, taking them out occasionally and fingering them just to feel the pain. They treat them like a comfortable old friend. We are not responsible for what was done to us as a child, but we are absolutely responsible for how we deal with it now.

Additionally, the need for parental approval is so strong that we keep going back to that poisonous well time and time again, desperately hoping to someday get the cool, refreshing water that our soul needs. But it continues to be bitter and acrid, burning our mouth and throat as it scours deep inside. At some point we have to realize that the people who were supposed to have loved us unconditionally were incapable of it for a variety of reasons. As unfair as it may be, we will never hear the things we need to hear or get the love and nurturing from them that we deserve. At that point, we have to lower our expectations so that we do not continue to get hurt each time we reach out, hoping for different results. We have to find that love and support from other sources.

The challenge in healing our wounds and changing our lives is that willpower alone is not enough. Our past experiences are imbedded in our subconscious, and the snap decisions we make in times of stress come directly from our subconscious. Willpower requires a conscious act.

Unfortunately, the unconscious mind is much more powerful than the conscious mind, with over 200,000 times more processing capacity.[2] In my experience it takes time and great effort to "reprogram" our subconscious mind and change our learned behaviors. We can start by understanding the dynamics of an abusive family and how that influences our life.

Understanding Our Family Dynamic

To make changes in our future, it is important to understand our past. By recognizing the dynamics of the family we grew up in, we can change those dynamics—or at least find adaptations to make them healthier—in our new families. The challenge for many of us is, we can be away from home for many years, and as soon as we come back, we slip into our old childhood personas.

Roberta M. Gilbert, MD, in her book *The Eight Concepts of the Bowen Theory*, describes Dr. Murray Bowen's family system theory. According to this theory, a superior life course is based on rational thinking rather than feelings, which are transitory. This theory is based on the family as an emotional unit rather than the individuals who comprise the unit. It is also based on observations rather than what individuals think, feel, or say about themselves or others. The family emotional system operates as a unit affecting each of the family members.

In the nuclear family emotional system, when couples marry they develop strategies to deal with problems (some healthy, some not). These strategies are passed on to their children—often in the form of anxiety which moves easily from person to person in the group. There are two types of anxiety: acute and chronic. Acute happens daily as we get stressed out about something—for instance, we get reprimanded at work or cut off on the freeway. Chronic anxiety is the kind that stays with us in the background and was programmed into us during our early years.[3]

We all carry around with us a certain level of chronic anxiety from our family of origin that creates a background level of hormones, such as adrenaline and cortisol, within our bodies. People from highly dysfunctional families carry around large amounts of anxiety and stress (along with high levels of these hormones). When we marry, our new family creates different types of anxiety, which causes the release of different hormones, producing a "cascade" effect and stimulating hundreds of chemical interactions. Anxiety is additive, meaning each circumstance adds new levels of anxiety onto the anxiety we already carry around with us normally. Some unwanted side effects of this additional anxiety might include weight gain, susceptibility to infection, ulcers, and possibly aging effects on the brain (dementia). When people with these high levels of background anxiety experience an outside circumstance such as a business setback, an IRS audit, or even normal life changes, their anxiety escalates to a much higher level than normal, and they tend to respond to all situations with higher levels of anxiety.[4] Because families are a single unit, when one member becomes stressed, everyone feels anxious. Even attempting to resolve the anxiety creates anxiety of its own.

Differentiation

Differentiation is a term that psychologists use to describe the individuality force of the members of the family. The degree of individuality each member has depends on how fused they are in their family relationship. People in dysfunctional families tend to be on the lower end of the scale, meaning they are very fused with one another and easily impacted by each other's stress levels. People at the lower end of this scale are vulnerable to stress and take longer to recover from it. They live in a "feelings-based" world, where feelings dominate objective reasoning. Feelings are "truth" to them, regardless of the facts. In more fused relationships (the lower end of the scale), anxiety passes more easily between people. This causes people to react emotionally to stressful situations. When making decisions or confronting problems, they may agree or disagree with a course of action based on the relationship rather than on the facts or logical reasoning. This is also known as *groupthink*.[5] Webster's dictionary defines *groupthink* as "a pattern of thought characterized by self-deception, forced manufacture of consent, and conformity to group values and ethics." In dysfunctional families this might manifest itself in the "normal" family syndrome, where each member of the family is required to maintain the façade of normalcy to the outside world despite facts to the contrary.

People at the higher end of the spectrum are less fused in relationships, and so they tend to have better, less stressful relationships. In marriage, differentiation is the process by which each spouse maintains a healthy self-identity while developing an intimate, loving, bonding relationship with another. It is the ability to maintain your sense of self even when emotionally close to others. It helps prevent our wounds and baggage from interfering with developing deeper intimacy and more passionate sex with our spouse. But it also keeps us from becoming enmeshed in trying to fulfill our spouse's needs at the expense of our own well-being. Differentiation develops tenderness, generosity, and compassion in a relationship. It enables the person to keep from holding grudges and to recover quickly from arguments, while still maintaining one's individual needs and priorities. Differentiation is a lifelong process that shapes and grows an individual and helps a couple to maintain their uniqueness and still cleave together as one.[6]

I don't know about you, but the home I grew up in sounds like we were on the lower end of the spectrum. An important thing to remember about differentiation is that we tend to develop our level of differentiation in our teens and leave our parents' home at about the level of differentiation that they achieved. This level generally gets passed from one generation of a family to the next. Dysfunctional parents tend to pressure their children to behave the same way they do as a form of validating or regulating their own emotions. This keeps children from developing the ability to think, feel, and act for themselves.[7] I grew up in an alcoholic home where there were very strict rules regarding loyalty to the family (don't tell an outsider), autonomy (don't think you are better than each other by growing or challenging the status quo), and most importantly, parenting (the adults' needs were most important, so the children had to parent the parents). This certainly challenged my ability to expand my vision of the world and placed restrictions on how I was able to grow as an individual and together with my wife as a couple.

Since my wife and I both grew up in high-stress homes, we each had a ton of background stress and hormones in our systems. Combined with our own self-created stresses, it took us awhile to figure out what was going on and learn to effectively deal with these circumstances in a productive manner instead of flying off the handle during a crisis.

The second issue we need to understand regarding our level of differentiation is that it is hard to change. We tend to marry someone who is at the same level as us. While we like to *think* one spouse or the other is much more advanced emotionally, this is just not true. This factor requires both spouses to change together in this area in order to effectively achieve positive results.

So given all that, how can we now heal our wounds so we can change the family dynamics that were instilled in us as children? Education is the first step to making any change. Now that you know what happened and why, you can use the following information to help heal the different areas of your life and move forward into adapting new strategies to become an untoxic parent.

Understanding Our Wounds

Erik Erikson is known for his theory on psychosocial development of human beings. He developed his famous theory and the concept of identity crisis despite not having a degree in medicine or psychology. His theory focused on how social influences (trauma, abuse, divorce, etc.) contribute to personality throughout a person's entire lifespan. Below is a summary of his stages of psychosocial development and the needed outcomes from each stage:

Stage: Infancy (birth to 18 months)
Basic Conflict: Trust vs. Mistrust . . .
Outcome: Children develop a sense of trust when caregivers provide reliability, care, and affection. A lack of this leads to mistrust.

Stage: Early Childhood (2 to 3 years)
Basic Conflict: Autonomy vs. Shame and Doubt . . .
Outcome: Children need to develop a sense of personal control over physical skills and a sense of independence. Success leads to feelings of autonomy, failure results in feelings of shame and doubt.

Stage: Preschool (3 to 5 years)
Basic Conflict: Initiative vs. Guilt . . .
Outcome: Children need to begin asserting control and power over the environment. Success in this stage leads to a sense of purpose. Children who try to exert too much power experience disapproval, resulting in a sense of guilt.

Stage: School Age (6 to 11 years)
Basic Conflict: Industry vs. Inferiority . . .
Outcome: Children need to cope with new social and academic demands. Success leads to a sense of competence, while failure results in feelings of inferiority.

Stage: Adolescence (12 to 18 years—note: the age in this stage probably extends beyond 18 years today)
Basic Conflict: Identity vs. Role Confusion . . .
Outcome: Teens need to develop a sense of self and personal identity. Success leads to an ability to stay true to yourself, while failure leads to role confusion and a weak sense of self.

Stage: Young Adulthood (19 to 40 years)
Basic Conflict: Intimacy vs. Isolation . . .
Outcome: Young adults need to form intimate, loving relationships with other people. Success leads to strong relationships, while failure results in loneliness and isolation.

Stage: Middle Adulthood (40 to 65 years)
Basic Conflict: Generativity vs. Stagnation . . .
Outcome: Adults need to create or nurture things that will outlast them, often by having children or creating positive change that benefits other people. Success leads to feelings of usefulness and accomplishment, while failure results in shallow involvement in the world.

Stage: Maturity (65 to death)
Basic Conflict: Ego Integrity vs. Despair . . .
Outcome: Older adults need to look back on life and feel a sense of fulfillment. Success at this stage leads to feelings of wisdom, while failure results in regret, bitterness, and despair.[8]

As we go through each stage of life we either successfully achieve the "goals" of that stage or we don't (for the sake of simplicity let's think of it as sort of a pass/fail experience). Generally any trauma or abuse that happens during that time frame causes us to not pass the goal of that stage. For instance, if our caretakers do not provide us with the proper feeding and affection as a baby, we fail to develop healthy trust and become distrustful of people. Or perhaps we get nurtured well through the first three stages of life and develop trust, autonomy, and initiative, but sometime during the ages of six to eleven, we are sexually abused by a relative. That trauma causes us to develop a sense of inferiority during that stage of life.

Typically, once we fail to acquire the positive goal of a specific stage, it carries over to the ensuing stages and negatively impacts those stages as well. Short of some sort of positive intervention (counseling, etc.) we will continue to fail acquiring the positive attribute of each successive stage of life. Obtaining the goals from each stage appears to help facilitate the acquisition of goals from the next stage. So someone with a sense of inferiority from the school-age stage will likely experience role confusion in the next stage, isolate themselves, and fail to develop strong relationships after that, be less involved in the world as an adult, and finally end their life with deep feelings of regret, bitterness, and despair. That example perfectly sums up my observation of my parents' lives. Neither healed from whatever stage of childhood in which they were wounded and continued to fail at each successive life stage until they passed away as bitter, lonely, and angry people.

Here's how a woman who has operated homeless shelters described her observations:

> Through the years, I've worked with homeless men, women, and children. Many have stopped at some stage

of their life where they were traumatized. They tend to stay in that cycle. As a result, they are not able to function normally. I've learned that they seem to have a mentality that refuses to accept responsibility for their actions. They have an entitlement mentality because of their situation. It takes a long time to turn this around and to help them heal. It doesn't happen overnight or in a few weeks. It's a process that takes time and a lot of work.

The good news is that we can go back and heal or reverse the pass/fail from any and every stage of life. As an example, let's say that you have always felt ashamed your entire life but don't know why. A counselor might work with you to try to discover what happened to you in your toddler years to cause you to fail to develop healthy autonomy. They can then design exercises or "homework" to help you develop confidence and healthy self-esteem. Or perhaps you experienced sexual abuse as a teen. Suddenly, you are confused about your role (possibly even your sexual or gender identity) in life. Likely as an adult you struggle with understanding your roles as a man or woman, husband or wife, or parent. A counselor can help you go back to that stage and work on developing your identity to help eliminate your confusion.

After years of counseling, mentoring, and education, I remember the feeling of finally understanding my role as a man, husband, and father. I was suddenly "comfortable in my skin," so to speak. It gave me confidence in all areas of life, and I stopped being so isolated and threw myself into trying to help people and make the world a better place. Today I feel like I have some wisdom to offer the world and will go to my grave feeling good about the contributions I've made and the mark I will leave.

Additionally, as we reverse these setbacks in our development, we greatly improve the odds of not passing them along to our children. Sometimes just going through the process of healing ourselves can be a learning experience for our own children. Certainly, understanding these stages of development helps us to know what we need to be cognizant of as our children pass through those stages. It helps us to be intentional in our parenting instead of just reactive.

Body, Soul, and Spirit

When we are traumatized or suffer abuse, it affects all three components of our being: our body, soul, and spirit. The body equals our physical being, the soul is the emotional part of us, and the spirit is the spiritual aspect of our being. Generally, we focus on one of the three and think that will make everything all right. For instance, if we are suffering from depression, we can treat the body by eating healthy meals and getting enough sleep and plenty of exercise. But that only treats the symptoms of the illness, not the core. The emotional portion is treated with medication and counseling, which is also extremely helpful, but again only treats part of the issue. To fully heal, you have to address both of those issues (body and emotions) as well as the spiritual component.

Most spiritual communities such as churches tend to focus on just the spiritual aspect of our wounds. That's an important component, but it only addresses 33 percent of the problem. Furthermore we have a tendency in the church to say to people who are suffering wounds of this nature things like, "Just pray more," or "If you truly believed, you would be able to get over this." "Just forget it and move on" is impossible unless you get a lobotomy. Those statements are not only untrue, they are more destructive than helpful. Those of us in the church (especially teachers and leaders) need to take the example from James when he says, "Be quick to listen, slow to speak and slow to become angry" (James 1:19).

One man told me of meeting with his pastor and confiding in him that he had AIDS. His pastor got very angry and shouted, "How dare you bring that disease caused by your lifestyle into our church!" The man told me, "I tried to explain that I contracted the HIV virus when I was molested as a boy, but he wouldn't listen." When our "No" didn't stop someone from doing evil to us as a child, it only compounds our pain when people make assumptions about us as human beings.

Abuse (childhood or domestic violence) seems to be a taboo subject in the church and Christian community. I don't ever hear any sermons on it, and very few workshops and seminars (although Celebrate Recovery might count) are presented. Perhaps because it is such an uncomfortable topic, people tend to shy away from it in polite company. But I dare say a significant portion of any congregation is suffering from childhood wounds. We would find people more willing to accept and rejoice in the good news of the gospel if we made efforts to heal those core wounds.

One way to approach taking care of spiritual wounds from childhood abuse might be to treat them like a physical wound. What do we do when we have a gash on our leg? We clean it out, keep it clean, and if it is bigger than we can handle, we get help. What happens if we neglect one or more of those steps? The wound gets infected, right? What's true on the outside is also true on the inside. We clean our wounds by confessing our sins, praying to God for forgiveness, and asking that he will purify us of unrighteousness. (Keep in mind that if you were abused as a child, *you* were not the one who sinned.) We then keep them clean by forgiving those who have sinned against us. And if the wound is too big, we allow others to come into our lives who can give us counsel and pray for us. As Proverbs 27:17 says, "As iron sharpens iron, so one person sharpens another." But people are often reluctant to clean their wounds.

When I was a little boy, I remember visiting my uncle's house. Showing off, I jumped on one of my cousin's bikes and flew down a steep hill in front of their house. I was going full speed when I noticed a car coming out of an alley on a collision course with me. With no choice I dumped the bike on the asphalt. The end of the handle bar landed on my thumb, grinding it into the pavement as I skidded to a stop. When I limped into the house with a thumb that looked like hamburger, my mom immediately grabbed a brush and scrubbed all the gravel out of the wound. Over my loud wails of protest, she then took and slathered it in Merthiolate. Hopping around blowing on it, I vowed never again to report an open wound. While the wound was painful, the cure seemed worse.

The same goes for those of us who have been wounded in childhood. We don't seek help because we think the cure is worse than the problem. We've already been badly hurt, why suffer pain again? Make no mistake about it, healing and change are hard. It's painful, takes a long time, and requires courage and fortitude. But if we take a holistic approach, it is easier and less painful in the long run to get through the process. We need to suffer the pain again, because if we don't, we will never be happy and we will likely pass on negative behaviors to our children.

Honoring Your Father and Mother

Of the Ten Commandments, the one abused people struggle with most is the one that instructs us to "honor your father and your mother." How do you honor a parent who hurt you physically, caused great emotional suffering, or sexually assaulted you? Let's look at some ways that make this possible.

One way to honor your mother and father—especially when they have not been honorable people—is by recognizing the good things they did (I know, but bear with me). They taught you those things even if that was not their intention. For instance, if you lived with alcoholics like I did, as the oldest child, I pretty much had to raise the other younger siblings a lot of the time. Hence, I learned a lot of skills that helped me later in life. I learned responsibility, I learned to be organized as well as self-sufficient, and I developed character from my suffering. I also learned practical skills such as how to launder clothes, cook food, wash the dishes, vacuum the floor, and polish the furniture. I was also forced to earn my own money for clothes and other things, so I learned to start and operate several businesses as a very young man. Having a paper route and a lawn-mowing business at age twelve taught me the fundamentals of small business ownership, which have served me my entire adult life. It taught me the value of hard work and the rewards of perseverance. Finally, having the courage as a child to reject my parents' lifestyle caused much abuse to be heaped upon my shoulders. But that courage has given me the opportunity to try new things that many people are afraid to attempt, such as starting my own businesses, writing books, and speaking in front of large crowds.

Additionally, there were good things my parents did (it wasn't *all* bad). They kept a roof over our heads (as tumultuous as it was inside). I don't remember ever going hungry, even though the meals often left much to be desired. And when not drinking, which wasn't very often, they could be fairly decent people.

Nevertheless I struggled for years on how to fulfill this commandment. Finally a pastor friend explained how he believed we could honor parents who didn't deserve to be honored. He said if we led lives that were honorable, if we were honorable people, we honored our parents. This was a huge epiphany for me. I knew I could lead an honorable life, one that would bring honor to my parents—if they were willing to accept it (which they weren't). But whether or not they recognized the gift I was offering them is not the issue. My actions met the requirement of that commandment when I was unable to fulfill it any other way.

As the survivor of abuse, you learned certain survival skills that are helpful in your life today. While the scarred-over wounds (or even raw ones) you carry around today may not feel like they were worth the effort, they make you who you are. I've had many people ask me if I wish my childhood had been better. I tell them, "No." While I didn't enjoy those experiences, the things I went through in childhood allow me to relate to other people who have gone through similar issues. They made me who I am. I would not be able to be used by God to touch the lives of many, many people if I had not had those experiences. The challenges you've been through have developed a part of who you are—often the best parts. If we are willing, God can use our worst wounds to minister through us to others.

My wife and I have had several discussions over the years about what our lives might have been like had we had healthy, loving parents who encouraged us and taught us the skills to succeed in life. Where would we be? What would we have accomplished? What kind of potential might we have had that was wasted? What would it have been like to have enjoyed an innocent, carefree childhood? We rued the loss of who we might have been, given the advantages of good parents and a loving home life. But then one day I came across an idea that completely changed the way I looked at this issue. In her book *Get Out of That Pit*, author and speaker Beth Moore addresses this very issue. Here's what she says: "I could tell Keith [her husband] was lamenting the potential he might have had if life had not tailspun him in a different direction. . . . 'Honey,' I responded, 'you're a much neater person *healed* than you would have been well.'" She goes on to say to all of us, "You have the capacity to be a ten times neater person healed than you would have been just plain well. Your wealth of experience makes you rich. Spend it on hurt people. They need it so badly."[9]

God can use your childhood abuse to do great things and you can too. There's the saying about making lemonade out of lemons. If you turn your negative experiences into positive ones by using them to help others, you have given them value.

4

Action Steps to Healing

> Healing may not be so much about getting better, as about letting go of everything that isn't you—all of the expectations, all of the beliefs—and becoming who you are.
>
> —Rachel Naomi Remen

Now that we have addressed some of our internal wounds, what are some practical steps we can take to start changing our lives? I spent (wasted) many years trying to conquer the world and slay my own demons before finally finding healing. The following are some ways that I found effective in overcoming my background. These steps are not necessarily in order or independent of one another. And these are certainly not the only ways to gain mastery over your past, but they were helpful for me. Some steps may work better for you in a different order than I've listed them and certainly some steps will overlap with one another. Regardless, you must do something or you will never find healing and peace of mind.

Education—Cause and Effects

When we have been traumatized (by anything), we develop certain survival techniques that seem logical to us even when we perform them unconsciously. Betrayal is a huge factor in the wounds we receive from childhood. When the people on whom we should be able to depend unconditionally for love, shelter, affection, nurturance, and training betray us, it creates jagged wounds that keep us from trusting and even loving others. Wounded people tend to exhibit several common characteristics, including holding on to their pain, trying to go it alone, being afraid to be vulnerable, not getting help, resisting change, and never expressing their hurt or anger (understandable if you were punished for expressing those emotions as a child). It takes courage to deal with our pain.

The first step to healing or change is to learn about what happened to our brain when we were traumatized. Read books, attend seminars and workshops, and watch videos on the topic. Once we have a basic understanding of what we are facing, many things that we are doing that may have confused us in the past suddenly fall into place. Once that happens we can begin to move forward and expand our education.

Support groups can be very helpful in our journey toward healing. There are a variety of adult survivor support groups. Adult Survivors of Child Abuse (ASCA) is an individual and group support program for adult survivors of physical, sexual, and/or emotional child abuse or neglect. If you have addictions, organizations such as Alcoholics Anonymous (AA), Narcotics Anonymous, or Al-Anon can be very beneficial. You can find support groups in your area in virtually any type of abuse you need help with.

I found attending an Adult Children of Alcoholics (ACOA) group to be very helpful. I'm not sure how I initially decided to go to a group like this, but I do know I wasn't very excited to go at first. In fact it took a great deal of courage. At the time, I wasn't exactly the kind of guy who was enamored with counseling and what I perceived to be "touchy, feely" kind of stuff like this. I think perhaps I just came to a point where I was so miserable that I knew if I didn't do something different, nothing was ever going to change, and I didn't want to spend the rest of my life being the kind of person I was. When I finally did go, the thing that was most insightful for me was discovering that there were people who thought and acted *exactly* like I did. I thought all of my problems were unique and no one else could possibly understand them. Imagine how refreshing it was to find a whole group of people who knew exactly what I was feeling and talking about before I even said it. It was like going through your entire life being nearsighted and one day putting on glasses—the whole world suddenly came into focus. This group and these people allowed me to discover a number of epiphanies about why I was responding to certain situations the way I was and how to deal with those situations in a more productive manner. It allowed me to grow to the next stage of my development and healing.

Most groups of this nature serve a specific short-term purpose. I observed some people who stayed in these groups for long periods of time rehashing the past and never moving forward. That seemed counterproductive to me, but I suspect each person has their own unique time frame of healing and development before moving forward (AA might be an exception to this).

At some point, we need to move on. Support groups alone will not heal you. Beth Moore comments, "If we keep patting ourselves on our broken backs, how will they ever mend?" [1] As Jesus said, "Can the blind guide the blind? Shall they not both fall into a pit?" (Luke 6:39 ASV).

The next step in your recovery needs to include professional counseling.

Counseling

Professional help is essential if you have been a victim of physical or sexual abuse. If you currently use drugs or alcohol to deaden your pain, you must deal with those issues first—you cannot gain control of your life if you are being controlled by an addiction. Addictions rule the actions and motives of a pain-filled soul.

The next stage of my healing process involved personal and couples counseling. At various times over the years, my wife and I attended counseling both as individuals and as a couple, sometimes concurrently, but most often one or the other. There were several things I learned from this process. First, it's very important to find the right counselor. For me, especially after becoming a Christian, I found it imperative to have a Christian counselor. Also, as a man, I felt it important that I saw a male counselor who could understand some of the challenges I faced that were unique to my gender. My wife also felt that seeing a woman was important for her for the same reasons.

Couples counseling was a bit trickier. We saw both male and female counselors during the process. We found it important to find one who respected both spouses. Frankly, that required us to go through a number of counselors until we found one who worked for us. For instance, several of the female counselors we saw in the beginning seemed to be putting the majority of the blame on me as a man (and all men). It may well have been true that I was the main problem in our relationship, but my wife, to her credit, was not comfortable or happy with someone who constantly pummeled me during our sessions, and we soon searched out other options. My relief, of course, was palpable.

I'm not sure age (or gender) matters regarding counselors, but I do know the two professionals I received counsel from who impacted me the most were both elderly men. One was a psychiatrist who taught me more in a year than I had learned my entire life—even though at the time I wasn't aware of it or appreciative of it. I continue to be blessed to this day by the time I spent with him as a young man. (One side note: this man was a Christian when I was not. He did not impose his belief system upon me but did gently guide me to understand some of life's truths from the Bible. My point is, I don't think seeing a Christian counselor even if you are not a Christian is a disadvantage.) I eagerly look forward to seeing him in heaven someday and thanking him for his wisdom. What joy it will be to tell him how my life worked out and the role he played in it.

If you have been abused, it is my opinion that a life coach or maybe even a pastor is not qualified to deal with these types of issues. You likely need someone who has had professional training in these specific areas to help you walk out the other side. Seeing a pastor in conjunction with a professional counselor may be a very appropriate approach though.

I periodically pay for a few "tune-up" sessions with a counselor just to make sure I am still on point and that my thought process hasn't gotten sidetracked. This also allows me to blow off some stress that might have built up and get some objective feedback on key issues that I am struggling with. If nothing else, this is reassuring, especially when I am mentoring and counseling other people and writing books to help people with these very issues.

Intense counseling requires hard work and lengthy dedication, and it's expensive. But it's part of the process necessary to heal. My wife and I chose to look at it as an investment in our future—and we're glad we did. Your kids will be glad you did as well.

Mentoring

No matter how dysfunctional our homes were—with no other examples to judge them against—we as children assumed they were "normal." But most of the people I talk to from abusive or even broken homes who have turned their lives around all tell me one very important item—at some time in their lives they all had a person, couple, or family who modeled for them what a healthy life looked like. It is extremely important to have that vision as a goal to look forward to and to provide hope. As humans we do not know what we do not know. If we are never exposed to a new "normal," we will continue to think the old vision that was modeled for us growing up *is* normal. This can be discouraging and defeating, not to mention destructive to our new family. Also, without that positive role model to replace the negative one, we might eliminate the old one but have only a void in its place. We fill that void with whatever we think is right, which may not work out so well. Without a vision for our future, we always return to our past.

Healing takes place in relationship—we cannot heal alone. When trust has been broken, you can't rebuild trust again except through another relationship. However, it's been my experience that broken people tend to take advice from other broken people, instead of from healthy people who could give them advice that would help. They do this because other broken people tell them the things they want to hear, and they feel comfortable around them—they think they "relate" to them. Of course following that advice is guaranteed to keep them in the same cycle of dysfunction they've lived in their entire lives. Additionally, it's difficult to have healthy relationships with broken people.

I was fortunate enough when I was twenty-four years old to meet my biological father (I spent time with him during my first two years of life but did not remember our time together). He had wanted to see me many times during my childhood but was thwarted by a vindictive mother. Over the years we have developed a close relationship. He is a good man and has made a difference in my life. Finally having a father who speaks blessings into my heart has been profoundly healing. The powerful father's blessings of "I'm proud of you" and "I love you" have healed many of the internal wounds I received early in life. He has been a positive role model of manhood, how a man conducts himself, and the life skills that I lacked growing up. His presence alone has been a major blessing in my life.

Without mentors we make plans, but they are generally unrealistic with little chance to succeed. If we've never been given the tools to lead a healthy life, we will eventually fall back on what we know from childhood. Those tactics do not work. One of the challenges I had as a parent was that I knew what I learned from my parents was not the model I wanted to use. But I didn't have any other example to replace that model with. I continued to struggle until I allowed people into my life whom I could observe parenting, talk with, and receive advice from.

My life changed 180 degrees when I had the courage to allow healthy (at least healthier than me) people into my life. That can be frightening for those who already feel unworthy, hopeless, or inadequate. We already judge ourselves harshly. We hesitate to admit our faults and open ourselves up to further criticism. People who have been abused tend to isolate themselves in order to maintain some semblance of control over their lives. The prospect of being criticized, lectured, or made fun of by someone who has their life "together" can be daunting. But I found the wisdom, encouragement, and healing I received was worth the gamble of allowing other people into my life. Actually none of those fears became true. Everyone I opened up to was very compassionate and helpful.

I actively searched out people who would be in my life and serve as mentors. That too can be frightening for anyone, healthy or not, because the fear of rejection is one of the primary fears of all humans. Generally, we think of a mentor as a respected confidant with whom we have a personal relationship. But mentors might also be someone whose counsel and teaching we study from a distance. I learned so much about being a man, husband, and father from my first pastor, Stu Weber. He taught me so much through his books and sermons without ever talking to me directly. He was a mentor to me and didn't even know it. I also learned so much about marriage and parenting from other great writers and speakers who served as "remote" mentors for me.

As a parent, I found that meeting with a group of men through our church was essential for me to become a better dad. Men I respected could say things to me that I might not have received very well from my wife or other people. Things like, "You are wrong on this issue," or "You are out of line here." They also provided collective wisdom on various strategies that worked or didn't work as parents in specific situations. They had been through circumstances that I had not, which gave me insight as to how to handle myself if I did find myself in one. Finally, having men to talk with gave me an outlet to talk about things that only another man can relate to.

Women likewise need a group of friends to talk with about things men aren't interested in or can't understand. They need to be able to fulfill their natural need for socialization and community. One of the problems for people who have been abused early in life is that we tend to isolate ourselves (as was modeled by our parents). But we need other people in our lives. Women especially need other women to talk with, relate to, and befriend.

Because of my wife's background, she has been affected with several issues over the years, not the least of which is those wounds inflicted upon her by her mother. Thankfully, there have been several older women who have stepped into the gap to help assuage that wound.

Due to an abusive home life, Suzanne left home at age thirteen, basically living on the streets. All the while, she was being raped by an older boy who claimed her as his property, and by fourteen, she had become pregnant. She gave the baby up for adoption and started attending high school again. While there, she met a young home economics teacher with whom she bonded. This teacher, Mrs. S, was only in her life for three months but made a big impression before Suzanne left that school. She genuinely cared and had compassion for her when no one else seemed to, and Suzanne says she felt that Mrs. S made her want to be a better person. It's kind of unexplainable, but Mrs. S somehow planted a seed of accountability that made Suzanne want to live in such a way that Mrs. S would be proud of her someday.

Suzanne lost track of Mrs. S as the years went by but not that seed, that connection. One day about fifteen years ago, we were on top of the building in which I had offices in downtown Portland, watching the Rose Festival Parade. As the tens of thousands of people marched by, my wife suddenly called out from the top of the five-story building, "Hey! That's Mrs. S!" Sure enough she was in a large marching band playing her instrument! Suzanne yelled, "Mrs. S! Mrs. S!" Mrs. S looked up, smiled, and shouted above the din, "Hello, Suzanna!" How either recognized the other after all those years seemed like a miracle. They soon reconnected and have stayed in loose contact since.

Several years ago, Mrs. S's treasured husband passed away, and we have had her over for Thanksgiving and for other events since. Our young adult daughter has adopted Mrs. S as a surrogate grandmother, and they spend time together sewing dresses and talking about important things for a young woman to know from a very proper older lady. Recently, just before Suzanne's birthday, Mrs. S called and asked if "Suzanna" could come over and visit her. During the visit,

Mrs. S shared that she remembered during Thanksgiving years ago that Suzanne did not have a set of good china. She wanted her to have her set (a very elegant set). Then Mrs. S shared that she also did not want Suzanne to get stuck with a broken car (as had happened last year) and that she had set aside money to give her a gift of a new car for her birthday. Despite Suzanne's protestations, they went to the dealer, and Mrs. S paid cash for a brand-new Subaru Outback with all the bells and whistles—safety features, leather seats, moonroof, etc. Suzanne stated emphatically that she did not need the leather or navigation system, but Mrs. S wouldn't let her leave without those "safety features." While Suzanne has had new cars before, they were always family cars—not hers alone.

Suzanne shed many tears of joy and elation over this unbelievable gift. Her co-worker said, of all people, Suzanne truly deserved this amazing blessing. Having watched Suzanne count pennies for ministry and milk and heard the travel tales of the past seventeen years, her colleague said, "Wow, wouldn't that feel amazing to be able to bless someone so deserving?" Suzanne said she didn't "feel" deserving, but her colleague said, "That's because you're a Christian, there are no expectations, but look how God works! Congratulations!"

But here is the truly awesome part. While the financial gift is generous beyond belief, I think Mrs. S gave her an even bigger gift. Because of her childhood, Suzanne entered life with several wounds—fatherless wounds, abandonment wounds, and mother wounds. As a man I have been able to help with some—the fatherless wound by providing, protecting, and loving her. The abandonment wound by being faithful and committed for thirty-four years. But I cannot address the mother wound—only another older woman can. I think

Mrs. S's gift of unconditional love (one that only a mother could and should give) will help to heal that mother-wound hole she has in her heart. I am already starting to see some exciting changes take place. I am so interested to sit back and watch what happens as she moves forward.

Other people can be long-term or short-term mentors. When our children were small and she was struggling with what it means to be a mother (primarily because she never had it modeled for her), Suzanne was blessed to have a woman come into her life and model what it meant to be a competent, loving mother and wife. She was a tremendous blessing in the short time she was in Suzanne's life—one that is still paying dividends.

As I've gotten older, I have searched for a mentor who has walked the same path I have of being a writer, speaker, and ministry leader. It's a tough and often lonely path that most people do not have experience with. I spoke about this with a pastor friend of mine who counseled me that I would never find a mentor who could fulfill all those roles for me. But he said I could find different mentors for each of the different areas of my life. I could find someone who could give me spiritual advice, someone for parenting, one for marriage, and others for my career. That seemed much less intimidating and has worked out pretty well.

My point is, no one succeeds in life without help.

Confronting Our Abusers

Many therapists do not believe in confronting your parents as a means of healing. They believe it doesn't heal wounds but reopens them. People tend to want to confront their abusers for a variety of reasons, mainly to get them to admit their shortcomings, to apologize for their misdeeds, and to gain some closure to move on with life. However, it's highly unlikely that an abusive parent or codependent parent is going to admit to their abuse. More likely they will deny it, blame the victim, or get very angry—often all three.

However, there may be some valid reasons for confronting your parents even if you do not get the justice you desire. Sometimes confrontation works. Now that you are an adult, the perpetrators no longer have any physical power over you. That revelation is often healing in itself. In addition, what we keep within ourselves, we allow to gnaw away inside us. And by "owning" the fear, guilt, shame, and anger they imposed upon us, we run the risk of passing it along to our children. Any time we do not resolve issues like this, they tend to get passed along to our children.

If you do decide that confronting your abusers is the way to proceed, you might start with a letter. Here are some things the confrontation letter should contain:

This is what you did to me.

This is how I felt about it at the time.

This is how it affected my life.

This is what I want from you now.[2]

If the purpose of confronting your parents is to be heard and get some things off your chest, a letter might serve that purpose. If you want to mend a relationship, then a face-to-face meeting may be required. The problem with this is that

Four Requirements
before Confronting Your Parents

- You must be strong enough to deal with their rejection, denial, and anger toward you.
- You must have a sufficient support system in place to help you through the anticipation, confrontation, and aftermath.
- You must have written down and rehearsed what you want to say and practiced nondefensive responses.
- You must no longer feel responsible for the bad things that happened to you as a child.[3]

most abusers (and those who allow them to abuse) never admit their actions. They try to twist it around to place the blame back on you. If you want to be heard in either situation, it's probably important to edit your language. An accusatory tone will cause the offending party to get defensive and push back. My wife sent a letter to her mother documenting all the horrible things she had either perpetrated upon her or allowed to happen to her as a child. It was well thought out and well written. Unfortunately, at the end of the letter she used a word she shouldn't have. Her mother was offended by that word and ignored all the relevant content. It was a very unsatisfying experience for Suzanne. Keep comments focused on how *you* feel, not how *they* should feel.

I would encourage you to talk with a trusted counselor and/or loving family members before trying to attempt a confrontation. It's not to be taken lightly, as much more damage can occur if it is not entered into properly.

Using Our Pain to Help Others

Using our pain, wounds, and damaging experiences to help others turns them from something rotten into something good. It gives them value. It takes a negative and turns it into a positive. Your experiences allow you to relate to others who have been through similar experiences in ways that other people never can. Your experiences of overcoming abuse give you the privilege of relating to other survivors so much more deeply than even the smartest psychologist can who has never experienced those types of trauma. (Note: We have to heal from those wounds first before we can start giving advice to others. Otherwise it is a case of the blind leading the blind.)

The quickest way to continue to heal your pain is to use it to start helping others—to bring good out of your pain. You can do this by helping mentor someone less healed than you, coleading support groups, speaking to groups large or small, or just befriending someone who needs your help. You can write about your experiences and what you've learned in any number of venues, from blogs to magazine articles to books. What you know, what you've learned, and what you've experienced can help someone in ways you can't even imagine. I frequently get emails and letters from people around the world who have read one of my books or heard me speak. They share how something I have said or written was life-changing to them. I am always stunned by this, because I don't consider myself all that brilliant. Clearly God uses my efforts well beyond anything I am capable of.

God's redemptive power is that he can use my pain to help heal others. It gives that pain meaning and value. And when I allow myself to be used in that way, it miraculously heals me as well.

5

Healing Our Emotions

Poisonous relationships can alter our perception. You can spend many years thinking you're worthless. But you're not worthless, you're unappreciated.

—Steve Maraboli

Emotions are an instinctive state of mind derived from our circumstances, mood, or relationship with others. They are feelings, which are inherently different from reasoning or knowledge. They arise within us spontaneously rather than consciously. Emotions seem to rule our daily lives. We make decisions based on whether we are happy, angry, sad, bored, or frustrated. We choose activities and hobbies based on the emotions they incite. The six basic emotions universal throughout all human cultures are fear, disgust, anger, surprise, happiness, and sadness.

Different people experience different emotions from the same event. Getting married or having a child can elicit emotions ranging from joy to anxiety. One movie scene that I show at my speaking events is pretty emotional. Most women who watch it shed tears of either joy or sadness, depending upon their backgrounds. When I show it to men in prison, most of them laugh at it (though that may be a defense response, because showing vulnerability in prison can be dangerous).

Emotions are also subjective. In other words, anger can encompass a range of levels from mild irritation to blinding rage. Love can range from brotherly friendship to blind adoration. We can feel a variety of emotions all at the same time. We can be excited and nervous at a job interview, or sad and happy that our child is going off to college. We can even experience conflicting emotions at the same time. It's possible to love and hate a person simultaneously, or to be both proud and disappointed in someone.

Our emotions are a fundamental part of who we are and how we respond to different situations. To those who have been abused in childhood, those emotional responses are often broken or at least warped. We need to address some of the emotions we have as a result of our backgrounds so that they do not rule our behavior, especially as it impacts our parenting.

Here are a few examples you might find helpful.

Attitude

Our attitude plays a big role in overcoming the challenges from our past. We can't control a lot of what happens to us in life, but our attitude is one thing we can control. One woman described it this way:

> I want to be gracious and forgiving, but it is hard. We know now that we suffered because we had bad parents, so I think, *Looking back feels worse than when we were going through it.* We deserved better. Today my heart hurts because I don't know that I was loved so much as tolerated and even that only lasted until I was 15. The absolute lack of love, support, and acceptance affected me to my core in a lack of self-esteem, confidence, social grace, the ability to forgive, and I live with a constant fear (of I don't even know what). What I did get from really crappy 15 years was the knowledge that I had to take care of me. I made a lot of bad decisions but at least I had the good sense to learn from them. I try to look at who I am vs. who they were. Two horrible, miserable, selfish unhappy people turned out a couple of pretty good, moral, hardworking people with wonderful, loving supportive families. Hard to be unhappy about that. Here is the other thing—it could have been a whole lot worse. People do really, really, really bad things to their children. As bad as it was, I am grateful our parents were not those people.

People have tremendously resilient temperaments that allow them to overcome early disadvantages. Author and columnist David Brooks comments, "Even among people who are sexually abused as children, roughly a third show few serious aftereffects in adulthood."[1] Perhaps it's because those people chose to take control of their attitude in life.

Part of having a good attitude is developing gratitude for what we have. Do you have a faithful spouse and children who love you? Then you are blessed beyond words. Be grateful. Do you have a home to live in and food to eat every day? Are you physically healthy? If so, you are better off than most of the people in the world. Be grateful—rejoice in the blessings you have been given. If you are reading this book, you must be educated. What a huge blessing! That means you can change yourself. Be grateful for what you do have, not unhappy about what you lack.

I do understand that it is not easy to force ourselves to be happy. I don't suggest this cavalierly. But our attitude is one of the few things we have control of. It is the one thing in life no one can take away from us. It's a mental discipline that gets stronger, like a muscle, as we exercise it. You can start improving your attitude and becoming grateful by regularly telling the people you care about how much they mean to you. Say "thank you" a lot (even if you don't really feel it at the time). Write down several things each day that you are grateful for, even if it's a stretch. Then think about some things that you like about yourself. Look in the mirror (even if it's difficult) and tell yourself some things you like about yourself. Pray for God to reveal all of the things he finds glorious about you. Do these things daily until you start to believe the truth about yourself.

Our attitude determines our level of satisfaction, happiness, contentment, and even our physical and mental health. We can choose to be dour and bitter, or we can choose to be, if not happy, at least grateful for the gifts we have. That attitude of gratitude goes a long way to changing our perspective on life and determining what kind of parent we become. Would you rather be a depressed, angry, scared parent or, instead, one who is happy, gracious, and loving? Me too.

Mourning and Grief

Another emotion that we have to deal with in order to heal is grief. Because many abused people have frozen emotions, they never grieve or mourn for their loss. Grief is a normal response to loss—in this case the loss of a normal childhood, our innocence, or even the love of a parent. We have to learn to mourn for the loss of good feelings about ourselves, loss of trust, loss of joy, loss of feelings of safety, and loss of nurturing and respectful parents. Grief and anger are intertwined. It's impossible for one to exist without the other.[2]

We also have to grieve the loss of the parents we hoped and yearned for. If Dad was abusive and Mom allowed him to be (or vice versa), they were both abusers. One of a parent's main jobs is to protect their children. To fail to do that or pretend they didn't know the abuse was happening is every bit as bad as actually performing the abuse. We have to mourn the fact that we will probably never get the love and nurturing that we needed (and rightfully should have an expectation of) and that our parents will probably never acknowledge and apologize for their actions. Abusive parents are incapable of this because they are either mentally ill, wounded, angry, weak, self-centered, or just plain evil. And if they have passed away, you will never get the justice or apology you deserve.

That may sound depressing, but it doesn't mean that you cannot get the things you desire from other sources. Likely you have a loving, supportive spouse and children who love you unconditionally. In addition you may have other family members (in-laws, grandparents, siblings, etc.), friends, or mentors who also love you and speak nourishment into your soul. Cherish those relationships and be grateful for what

Common Stages of Grief

Early Stages

Shock—experiences numbness, denial

Emotional release—begins to feel pain and hurt

Preoccupation with deceased or loss—keeps thinking about loss or events

Anger—feels abandoned or powerless

Depression/sadness

Symptoms of Physical and Emotional Distress

Sleeplessness	Poor appetite
Tightness in throat	Sense of unreality
Choking or shortness of breath	Emotionally distant— no one cares or understands
Hollow feeling in stomach	Feelings of panic or desire to run away
Weakness	

Latter Stages

Dialogue/bargaining	Acceptance
Forgiveness	Return to life

These are common stages, not required ones; they are not predictable, linear, or universal.

you do have. Some people are not fortunate enough to have anyone who cares about them.

One of the challenges of dealing with wounds from abuse is that we have to process our grief. An unfortunate side effect of abuse, however, is that many abused people cannot feel anything—our emotions are frozen. We had to learn to put our emotions in a box in order to survive. Most abused children are punished for expressing their feelings. So it likely wasn't safe to have feelings in childhood, or they were so painful that we pushed them away in order to cope.

The process of working through grief and starting to feel those emotions again is painful. It takes time and cannot be hurried. There are several stages of grief that we must work through in order to come out the other end. We typically only associate grief with the death of a loved one. But in the case of an abusive childhood, the grief is caused by the loss (figurative death) of never having had a loving, nurturing parent-child relationship—the death of childhood innocence and a happy childhood.

Two months before Suzanne and I married, my baby sister was killed in a car accident. It was a shock to all of us, but my parents, being unable to handle life in the best of times, completely fell apart. As the oldest child, it was left up to me to handle all the funeral arrangements. Probably due to the way I had been programmed growing up (or the limited life skills I had at the time), I ended up stuffing my emotions in order to do what had to be done. Unfortunately, by the time the dust settled, those emotions stayed stuffed deep down inside me. I never properly processed my grief and instead moved on with my life. But those unprocessed emotions eventually have to come out. They can only stay smashed inside like a sleeping bag in a stuff sack for so long before the seams weaken and they explode out. When my feelings did finally come out, they were so much more painful to deal with. It took longer and was more difficult than if I had dealt with them earlier in life.

As frightening as it may be to think about dealing with your grief, please know that the sooner you do it, the sooner you will be well. You will benefit from a good counselor to help you through this transition.

Dealing with Our Anger

Most people who have been abused are angry—rightfully so. It's okay to be angry—you have a right for some amount of anger, given what's been done to you and the lost innocence of your childhood. However, you do not have the right to allow that anger to pass on those wounds to the important people in your life, like your spouse or children. Hence we have to learn to deal with our anger in a healthy way in order to keep it from contaminating those around us.

For some people with abusive childhoods, anger is often frightening—when exhibited both by others and by themselves. You were likely punished for being angry as a child. Plus the people who abused you were likely very angry, and that was frightening as a child. Anger also has the potential to destroy people. To wounded people, getting angry means losing control—and control is something they cling to like a life vest in rough seas. Anger can be a very complicated emotion for victims of abuse on several different levels.

Wounded people often deal with anger in one of several ways—they bury it and become sick or depressed, or they deaden it with things like alcohol, drugs, sex, or food. Sometimes we allow our internalized anger to turn us into bitter, frustrated, belligerent people. Other people just run around

Ways to Deal with Anger

- Give yourself permission to feel the emotion of anger—i.e., put a name on it.
- Externalize your anger. Instead of turning it inward, express it constructively in healthy ways. Talk to people about it, punch pillows, etc. Expressed anger gives you energy, repressed anger is draining.
- Increase your physical activity. This releases tension as well as produces endorphins, which enhance your sense of well-being.
- Use your anger as motivation for life change. I used my anger productively to make life changes to ensure I would never be like my parents. Don't allow your anger to reinforce negative self-images. You are not a bad person because you feel anger. Anger is a logical and reasonable response for what has happened to you.[3]

wielding their anger like a flame thrower, with a scorched-earth policy toward everyone around them.

It takes time to deal with anger issues. Women especially have been socialized not to show their anger. This often leads them to turn their anger inward, which causes them to act in self-destructive ways. Eating disorders, self-harm (cutting), self-medicating with drugs or alcohol, shopping, promiscuity, smoking, or hoarding might all be symptoms of internalized anger in females. Or they choose partners who can act out anger for them, thus releasing their repressed anger vicariously. Unfortunately these kinds of men (and women) are often controlling and abusive.

While females typically turn their anger inward, many males turn their anger outward, doing great damage to themselves and others. Here are some dynamics of anger in males.

Anger produces a physiological arousal in males. It creates a state of readiness and heightened awareness. It creates energy that can be directed outward in the form of protection or even as a weapon. Anger causes a fight-or-flight response designed to protect us. Anger is frequently a powerful tool boys and men use to cover our inadequacies. You'll notice that young and even older males will react with anger when they become overly frustrated or are hurt emotionally.

The surge of adrenaline and associated arousal can be addicting to some males. Young males need to be taught how to deal with and control their anger. In order to do that, they must learn to own their anger and identify the source of that anger. Then they can learn to determine how to choose to respond to their anger. Likely, we will need help to be able to identify the source of our anger, either through a counselor or a loving family member. My wife was instrumental in helping me learn what I was feeling at any given time and why. She was much more in touch with and knowledgeable about emotions. This allowed her to talk with me (after I was done being angry) about what I was really feeling.

Males are not very adept at understanding their emotions nor very comfortable dealing with them. Emotions are powerful and often uncontrollable. That's why many males keep such a tight lid on their emotions—once released they are difficult to predict or control and often result in a situation ending in vulnerability. The one emotion, however, that they are relatively comfortable with is anger. Anger for many men is an old friend, one they call upon in a variety of circumstances. Like all powerful emotions, it can be used destructively or for good. For instance, anger can be terribly destructive in relationships. All we need to do is look at the devastation caused to women and children through a man's uncontrolled wrath and anger. Anger can lead to emotional, psychological, and even physical abuse.

On the other hand, anger *can* be channeled into productive pathways. Anger can be used to motivate a man to achieve more than he might otherwise be able to accomplish. It can be used as a mechanism to encourage perseverance under duress or in grueling circumstances. Many a boy accomplished some difficult task all because he got angry when someone told him he couldn't succeed. When teased, many boys use that anger to motivate themselves to "prove" their offenders wrong. One method in coaching is to get young men angry in order to motivate them to perform beyond their self-imposed limitations. In fact, many men—myself included—propel themselves with anger and grit to succeed in life because a father figure constantly told them they wouldn't amount to anything. Warriors often use anger toward their enemies as motivation to succeed in battle or even in a school-yard fight.

Regardless of how it is used, anger is the emotion most familiar to males. Anger is often a secondary emotion used by males to cover or mask other emotions. For instance, certain emotions such as fear, anxiety, vulnerability, or distress often produce a feeling of humiliation in males. Humiliation is considered a weakness by males. Remember, for most males to show weakness is to be vulnerable and open to criticism. To be vulnerable is an invitation to be attacked. But anger is a defense against attack and may even be a weapon to attack others. Very angry men and boys are seldom messed with, even by bullies. I can remember using anger as a defense mechanism just to keep people away from me. After my childhood I just wanted to be left alone.

Rather than feel humiliated by these "unmanly" emotions, many males instinctively and automatically use anger to cover those feelings. Even pain (physical or psychological) can be covered by anger. Notice how most males react when they hit their thumb with a hammer. They'd rather get mad than cry. Most men also get angry rather than depressed or hysterical when faced with an emotional crisis in a relationship. Again, this is a protective mechanism for their fragile egos—egos that are covering secretly ingrained feelings of inadequacy and incompetence.

Sometimes anger is even used consciously. I was raised in an alcoholic and abusive home. I distinctly remember at about the age of twelve when I first discovered that if I got angry, I didn't have to feel that humiliating emotion of being afraid. In typical naive boyhood fashion, I told myself, "This is great. I'll never be scared again!" However, this was a foolish hope, as I spent a significant portion of my adult life being angry. I didn't have a positive male role model to show me how a man lives his life and faces his problems in a healthy manner, so my default response was often anger. And that's a scary way to live life.

Forgiving Our Abusers

I hesitate to even bring this subject up because it is so painful to so many. Frankly, it even leaves a bit of a bad taste in my mouth just saying it. But it's too important not to discuss. We need to consider forgiving our abusers—there I said it. When they hear the word "forgiveness," most abused people think, *Why should I forgive them? I didn't do anything to deserve this. They are the ones who harmed me. They don't deserve forgiveness!* Those thoughts are understandable and maybe even justified. But there are some reasons to consider why forgiveness may be the most important thing you can do for *yourself*.

Is forgiveness of our abusers required in order for us to heal and move forward? Prevailing wisdom of the mental health industry and in much of the spiritual realm would say that it is. However, a growing number of psychologists and psychiatrists would say just the opposite. Part of the problem is that most abusers do not change. To forgive someone who is still engaging in destructive behavior and who refuses to admit their culpability for their actions and atone for them seems somewhat counterintuitive. Oftentimes people who have been abused are so eager and desirous to have at least some connection with a parent (even an abusive one) that they continue to try to get a different response from that parent. Unfortunately, ground chuck will never turn into filet mignon, no matter how much we yearn for it to be so.

Forgiveness consists of two aspects: letting go of resentment and giving up the need for revenge. The revenge part often isn't a problem—giving up the need for revenge is healthy and may even be easy. The first part is more difficult. Letting go of resentment can be very difficult, especially if the offending party is not repentant. But their apology or the changing of their behavior is not the point of forgiveness. You forgive others for the peace and healing it brings *you*.

One of the challenges of forgiveness is that we have to be careful it does not become a form of denial: "If I forgive you, we can pretend what happened wasn't all that terrible." Sometimes people rush to forgiveness to avoid the painful work of therapy. And in situations where the guilty party has never been held accountable for their crimes, absolving them of the responsibility for their actions may be more harmful than good. How are you supposed to "forgive" a parent who came home drunk and beat you bloody, or a father who raped you as a child? Forgiveness may also crimp your ability to release emotions. How can you be angry at a parent when you have already forgiven them? That anger then gets directed inward, toward ourselves, becoming even more destructive. Accepting blame is a survival tool for abused children. Part of overcoming that is recognizing and accepting who was responsible for your childhood pain. (Note: You are NOT responsible for any abuse you suffered as a child.) If you don't, you will continue to blame yourself and continue to suffer shame and guilt.

So is forgiveness necessary to heal and change your life? Probably. Certainly people will disagree with me on that issue, but my belief is that forgiveness is fundamental in order to heal and move forward. I believe that God would have us forgive our abusive parents, but I also believe it's important that forgiveness comes at the end of a lot of hard work, not at the beginning or in lieu of that hard work. Understand though that forgiveness does not mean we deny the other person's responsibility or justify their actions.

Sometimes in the church we are pressured to rush to forgiveness. This is spiritual abuse. Hurt people need a safe place to tell their story. They need people to stand beside them, sympathize with them, and be outraged for them. What they don't need are platitudes like "God must have a reason."[4]

Science has proven that forgiveness may be healthier for us than we know. Forgiving someone reportedly lowers blood pressure, decreases stress and fatigue, improves sleep, and decreases depression symptoms. When people are able to forgive, they are empowered.[5]

Doctors are recognizing that patients who refuse to forgive often stay sick. Pastor and author Dr. Michael Barry says, "Harboring these negative emotions, this anger and hatred, creates a state of chronic anxiety." He continues, "Chronic anxiety very predictably produces excess adrenaline and cortisol, which deplete the production of natural killer cells, which is your body's foot soldier in the fight against cancer."[6] Not forgiving others causes people to get sick and keeps them sick. Of all cancer patients, 61 percent have forgiveness issues. Forgiveness therapy is now being looked at as a way to help treat cancer.[7]

Personally, I found that at least some level of forgiveness *was* required by me in order to heal and move on to live a decent life. That doesn't mean that I absolved my parents of their guilt, but I gained some understanding of why they acted the way they did, and that allowed me to have the compassion to accept their faults as wounded human beings. For instance, my stepfather was a weak and twisted man in many ways. But for all his faults, he was a better man and father figure than his father was. He was also less abusive than his old man. I came to realize that his abuse was probably not so much based on malice as it was on ignorance. I sincerely doubt he had much of a clue about how his own legacy contributed to his behavior as an adult, and he probably became an alcoholic in order to live with himself. He probably also became one in order to live with my mother.

My mother was a wounded soul from childhood abuse and incest. For whatever reason, she chose to self-medicate with alcohol her entire adult life rather than have the courage to face her wounds and try to heal them through counseling and medication. This doesn't excuse what she did to me and my siblings, but it does make it more understandable. But understanding why people do what they do does not make it any more acceptable. However, it did allow me, at the end of my mother's life, to have the compassion to help facilitate her passing with grace and dignity.

The forgiveness I extended to my parents who raised me was not for their benefit, it was for mine. Carrying around all that bitterness and pain is destructive to us on many levels. And frankly, your parents (or other abusers) probably don't care whether you forgive them or not. Forgiveness allowed me to move beyond emotions like shame, guilt, rage, and grief. Anger and resentment are poisons that hurt only us, no one else. If you have accepted Christ's forgiveness in your life, you have an obligation to forgive others as well. *Forgiveness is not weakness—it is power.* It gives us power over the situation instead of keeping us a victim. You will be well on your road to recovery when you can begin to forgive the people who have harmed you.

Forgiving Ourselves

Before giving my life to Christ, one of the biggest challenges I faced was not being able to forgive myself for some of the things I had done. This was a huge burden. It held me back in so many areas of life, including my parenting. One of the greatest joys that came from accepting Christ as my Savior was the relief I experienced when I felt God's forgiveness for the first time. I felt as if a giant hole had been mended in my heart and a granite weight had been taken off my back.

Most people who come from troubled backgrounds struggle with forgiving themselves (maybe even people who *don't* come from troubled backgrounds struggle with this issue as well). Some of the things they feel bad about are legitimate, some are misguided, and some are outright lies told by people who should have loved us. These lies are then perpetuated by forces that love to see us mired in misery.

The evil one is a liar. He knows that deep in our hearts we are so fragile and injured by life that the faintest whisper will make us feel guilty even when we are not. He knows the hardest person for us to forgive is ourselves.[8]

Remember, your past is not your future. A bad history is not your destiny. But it's hard to love others when we don't love ourselves. One of the challenges in forgiving ourselves is that we tend to set the bar too high—we demand perfection from ourselves. When we don't achieve it, we believe that we are bad or somehow irredeemably flawed.

We talked earlier about the physical toll that unforgiveness places on the human body. Unforgiveness of oneself is just as onerous. We seldom extend to ourselves the same grace we extend to others. Forgiving ourselves means we realize we are not perfect. We all make mistakes but we are not the sum of our mistakes—they do not define us. I was much harder on myself than I was on other people (although there are those who would say I was just plain hard on everyone).

But what most people failed to realize was, I beat myself up way more than I ever would someone else.

Forgiving others and forgiving ourselves takes time and hard work. I might never have accomplished it without God's intervention and forgiveness in my life. The truth is, you really do deserve forgiveness. Without forgiveness the wounded becomes the wounder. When we have a difficult time forgiving ourselves, we have a hard time forgiving others (like our spouse and children). And they definitely deserve our forgiveness.

Faith and Hope

Finally, the most powerful healing agent is faith. To develop faith is to know hope. Without faith there is no hope. With no hope there is no reason to go on. Having the faith to believe in God's grace and forgiveness lets him heal our wounds and provide us with hope for the future—that even if our past has been ugly, our future is bright. Listen to me—God did not allow or cause our plight. He does not harm his children. He has given human beings free will. Faith means nothing if it is coerced. Therefore people can choose to follow God or choose not to (and accept the consequences). That means that some people have the freedom to choose to do harm to others. But even in our darkest times it doesn't mean God was absent. It's possible that he protected us from even greater harm. And in the bigger picture (which we cannot see), perhaps your wounds are a vital part of events that we cannot comprehend—such as being able to help someone else. There is much about God we cannot understand, and that's okay. Faith is believing even when we cannot see, hear, or understand the bigger scheme of things.

You have had a great injustice done to you. Without faith, hope is powerless—it's just a wish. But if it's true that one of God's attributes is justice and that we will all have to account for the lives we led, then you can have faith and hope that all your wounds (and the sins levied against you) will someday be redeemed.

I want to encourage you to allow God into your heart. Ask him to forgive your sins and have a relationship with you. The love and forgiveness you will experience will heal the holes in your heart that nothing else can. It is supernatural healing—it's unexplainable. God does love you and he wants to use you to help others. Give him a chance and see what happens.

6

New Parenting Strategies

I think that enduring, committed love between a married couple, along with raising children, is the most noble act anyone can aspire to. It is not written about very much.

—Nicholas Sparks

We are all the best parents we know how to be. And none of us are experts. Most parents aren't bad parents, they just lack parenting skills. Unfortunately, those of us raised in abusive homes know even less about healthy parenting than those with positive role models growing up. Part of that discrepancy is due to the way our brains developed because of the models we observed.

Your brain consists of billions of individual cells or neurons that develop 1,000 trillion connections with each other. An infant's brain at birth is only 25 percent developed, allowing it to adapt to many different environments. Hence, the brain of a child raised by loving parents will develop differently than one raised in a home with a drug-addicted mother and lots of domestic violence. Even if we do not consciously remember these childhood experiences, our brain still does. The primary job of the brain is survival. If survival is threatened, the rest of the brain shuts down except for the functions that help self-preservation. For a child in a violent home, the higher-functioning regions of the brain will become smaller (from lack of use), affecting the child's ability to learn and understand the world, other than how to survive by being ever-vigilant of possible harm. The good news is, we can change and develop these portions of the brain through plenty of positive reinforcement and nurturing.[1]

Part of changing our parenting strategies is to be intentional about our parenting *before* we find ourselves in situations that cause us to act out from our past programming. I remember an ugly incident from when my son was a baby. I was watching him one day while my wife was shopping. It had been a particularly stressful day, and I was worn out. Frank began crying and continued to cry vigorously in his crib no matter what I did for him. I just needed a few minutes of peace and quiet. Finally, at wit's end, I went in and snatched him up. I shook him and angrily yelled into his face, "Would you just shut up for a minute! Just shut up!" The shocked look of confusion and abject terror upon his tiny tear-stained face shamed me. He didn't know why I was upset, only that the person he was totally dependent upon was threatening him. I'm haunted by that memory to this day. It's a constant reminder to me of how easy it is to abuse the power God has endowed us parents with. I realize now as an older, experienced father, that if I had approached my fathering from an intentional perspective instead of just one of reaction governed by my emotions, I could have avoided potentially destructive situations like this. I vowed after that incident that I would take every step necessary to learn how to become a different kind of parent.

Changing our lives, becoming different than the examples that were modeled for us, takes great effort and focus. You have a lot of catching up to do. It's something you cannot do on your own. Yet, with help and healing like previously discussed, you can become a fantastic parent despite your upbringing. Remember—your past does not dictate your future. Here are a few things to take into consideration as you go forward.

Reprogramming Our Brain

One of the challenges of becoming a good parent when we didn't have one growing up is that our brain is programmed to think and act in certain ways during various circumstances. You find yourself instantly responding to specific situations in ways you have been programmed to from childhood. Often these are responses you would not choose to react with—many of us have what would be termed poor impulse control. For instance, in the alcoholic home where I was raised, a loud, unexpected noise was guaranteed to provoke a very angry, if not violent, response from a parent with a hangover. Hence, I was programmed to respond to a startling noise with a hyperdeveloped fight-or-flight response. As I became an adult, being afraid became unacceptable, so to this day I react to loud noises with an anger (fight) response. Even though I knew about it and explained this reaction to my children, it was not a healthy way to respond to a common occurrence in life. I have poor impulse control when startled. I've worked hard over the years to stifle my impulse to react this way. Coincidently, my children found it to be a fun game over the years to sneak up on Dad and startle him with a loud noise.

Why do we react this way? We've all at one time or another sworn to ourselves that we would never do things our parents did or say things they said, and then find ourselves saying or doing those very things under times of stress. Here's a brief explanation of what takes place in our brains and how we can change it.

Your brain consists of billions of neurons. Each neuron has dendrites that connect with potentially thousands of other neurons, relaying electrical impulses between them (communicating). When a specific connection is used enough times (for example, driving a car), it develops neural pathways that you use in those specific situations. These frequently used pathways eventually develop a layer of fat, called a *myelin sheath*, which allows them to operate at even faster speeds. This chain of neurons firing electrical connections directs the nervous system to take action. The nervous system responds by producing neurotransmitters (such as serotonin, dopamine, and norepinephrine), which allow each neuron's information to jump the synaptic gap between them and pass its message along to the other. Develop enough of these pathways during a specific activity and it becomes second nature (like riding a bike—we don't even have to think about it). Our brains become programmed in a specific way.[2] That's why we can drive home from work on the freeway and arrive with no conscious thoughts on how we got there. Or how we can dry ourselves when we get out of the shower without thinking about it. In fact, try consciously thinking about drying yourself (or change the order you do it) and see what happens—it's very awkward.

That's a brief and oversimplified explanation of how our brains work. But my point is that we learn various survival skills during childhood. Our brains become wired to survive in that environment. Especially in abusive situations, our brains are programmed to respond to various stimuli in ways that may not be appropriate once we are no longer in those stressful or dangerous environments. During our earlier discussion on PTSD, we saw how our sense organs in the brain look for a threat—it can be real or perceived—and order the neurotransmitters into action. If it's a perceived (not real) threat similar to something that happened in childhood, we can end up acting inappropriately. Unfortunately for people from abusive home environments, their danger detectors are often overly active warning systems. They warn too often and the warnings are too intense. That means that anything vaguely resembling a threat can appear catastrophic.

As an example, for whatever reason, there was a severe reaction to the spilling of milk at the dinner table when I was a child. With four small children at the table, you can imagine there was a lot of spilt milk going around. Later, I found when I had small children and they spilled milk, the same strong fear reaction was provoked within me. I had to reprogram my brain to not react the way my parents did when milk was spilled. This is an instantaneous, unconscious reaction and not one that is easily controlled by self-discipline. We have a surge of adrenaline before we even know what's happening. If we do not find a way to reprogram our brains, we run the risk of passing those dysfunctional and damaging programs on to our children. I must have been at least partially successful, because my grown children today think it's funny and give me grief about spilt milk nearly every time they visit.

Does that mean that once those neural pathways have been established in our brains we are stuck with them for the rest of our lives? Well, yes and no. The pathways do not go away, although they diminish the less they are activated (again using the example of riding a bike—we never forget how, we just get rusty at it after a long period of disuse). But the good news is, we can create new pathways. In fact, it's easier to create new patterns in our brains than to unlearn old ones (it would be really difficult to try to retrain ourselves to not know how to ride a bike). While it's not easy to change our brain patterns, it is doable because of the brain's plasticity. This is called *neuroplasticity*—"the brain's amazing lifelong ability to change how its neurons interact with each other."[3]

So how do we change destructive thought patterns and create positive ones? The more we use the neurons in our brains, the more they recruit other neurons to wire together to create neural pathways. As we saw earlier, the more these pathways are used, the more established they develop into patterns or habits. What does this look like from a practical standpoint? Let's say you had parents who were verbally abusive and were always angry and critical of you and everyone else. Not surprisingly, you grew up to be angry and critical of everyone around you. But now that you are a parent, you want your children to feel better about themselves than you feel about yourself. You don't want to treat your children the way your parents treated you, nor pass those traits on to them. You decide the way to do that is to offer praise every chance you get, instead of always finding fault. Every morning you remind yourself to offer praise and positive feedback to your children, and you do that several times each day. Gradually this becomes easier and, surprisingly, being critical becomes harder.[4] Eventually you don't even have to think about it anymore. Congratulations! You've just created new neural connections and networks in your brain.

At first, developing these connections is difficult and moves slowly, but with use and practice, the connections get more established and "fire" much more smoothly and quickly. Think of when you first started learning to play a musical instrument. At first it was painstakingly slow and difficult. But over time you got better (as your brain patterns developed), and it started being easier and you became more proficient. Sometimes there is even an "aha!" moment when something clicks and everything seems to fall into place. I've experienced that when playing sports. One minute I was inept at a skill and seemingly moments later I was a pro at it. Of course there was a lot of practice between the two stages, but that's how we develop neural networks within our brain. Unfortunately, this theory doesn't seem to work with golf for some reason.

You can do this too. You can reprogram new networks within the brain to replace the old patterns. This begins by having an idea of what you want to do differently. The idea causes you to reflect upon your behavior. This then causes you to repeatedly change those behaviors you don't like or institute new ones. You perform these new behaviors every day. (Note: It's not enough to want to stop old behaviors; you must have a positive behavior in mind that you want to replace it with.) That change in behavior slowly reshapes your neural networks until they are more biased toward your new way of thinking. Eventually, they become the rule rather than the exception, and you find that you have changed the way you behave—you've reprogrammed (or retrained) your brain. You can do this in many areas of your life.

Here's how a friend of mine said she helped reprogram the negative influences in her brain:

My father had an Archie Bunker mentality. He was a loud-mouth, a bigot, bad-tempered, and extremely disrespectful to his wife. He was very opinionated and loved to pick topics of conversation to prove and push his point of view, basically he loved to argue. With a fragile ego, he was often offended, depressed, and angry if criticized in any way. Whenever I repeated an action or phrase my father used to use, I would work out a plan to handle it in a more healthy way. Like the time when my three-year-old daughter threw a temper tantrum in a store, and I grabbed her hand, put my face right in front of hers, and said, "What's the matter with you? You stop crying and knock it off or I'll give you something to cry about!" Upon reflection, I hated what I had just done! It was what my dad had said and done to me my entire life. I wrote out a healthy plan to use if it ever happened again. I read it several times a day and carried it in my wallet so I would be ready. I ended up with plenty of practice because three-year-olds have a lot of tantrums. Every new stressful stage in my young adult life brought out the words and actions my father used. I had to constantly plan and work out new reactions. Over much time and with work, the fatherly "gut reactions" reduced, became infrequent, finally disappearing.

Understand, though, that retraining your brain requires dedication and repetition. You cannot go into it with a "half-way" mentality. You have to be dedicated and all-in. Much like trying to quit smoking or recover from substance abuse, half measures get you nowhere. If it's not a top priority, you won't see many results. Additionally, change takes time and effort. Your brain has developed some of its old patterns over a lifetime. You won't be able to change them overnight. I'm trying to quit eating sugar. I've eaten sugar for over half a century. It's been extremely difficult to change those old patterns in my brain (especially when I am not as all-out dedicated as I need to be).

Changing your thought process is difficult and takes time. But reprogramming your brain is the only way to make life-long changes in your behavior. Once you have accomplished this, you've taken huge steps toward breaking the negative generational cycles that have been passed down in your family. What better way to become a great parent, even when you didn't have one.

Decision Making and Unconscious Biases

We also have to be aware of how we have been unconsciously programmed, particularly in regard to our decision-making process. As mentioned earlier in this book, words spoken to us as children by the adults in our lives carry great weight. Those words stick with us and we believe what is said to us, even if it is not true. This causes us to make decisions based on faulty assumptions.

Heuristics is the theory that learning is influenced by our experiences and trial-and-error methods that shortcut the learning process and allow us (force us) to come to a quicker solution. Sometimes this is good and sometimes not so good. One example of this involves what is known as *priming*. You can prime people to make certain choices or act in certain ways just by the words or cues you use with them. For instance, if you use words like "bingo," "Florida," or "ancient" on a group of individuals, they will walk more slowly leaving the room than they did entering. Before a test, if you use words like "succeed," "master," or "achieve" in a sentence, the participants will perform better on tests. It works with negative stereotypes as well. Brooks says, "If you remind African American students that they are African Americans before they take a test, their scores will be much lower than if you had not reminded them. In one case, Asian Americans were reminded of their ethnicity before a math test. They did better. Then they were reminded they were women. They did worse."[5]

Imagine what kind of unconscious decisions and choices we make if people use words like "worthless," "stupid," or "loser" when talking to and about us while growing up. How might that affect the way we approach life and our level of success? Certainly they would produce unconscious biases within us that would probably cause us to act in self-destructive or limiting ways.

Another heuristic involves anchoring. An example of this is when stores manipulate our choices by influencing the value we attribute to a product. For instance, a $30 bottle of wine may seem expensive when surrounded by $9 bottles of wine, but it seems cheaper when surrounded by $149 bottles of wine (which is why wine stores stock those super expensive wines that almost nobody actually buys).[6]

One of the outcomes for people who have been abused is that they do not feel they are valuable—they do not value themselves. This often causes others to place less value on them as well. By comparing ourselves to the unrealistic image of us produced by our parents (or other abusers), we undervalue our lives. This is another reason to associate with healthy people (who place a higher value on themselves) rather than broken people (who likely undervalue themselves). By comparison we will feel better about ourselves. If we feel better about ourselves, our children will feel better about themselves as well.

Next is *framing*. This is when decisions are influenced by context. In this case, mental patterns are connected and judged in comparison to everything else. "If a surgeon tells his patients that a procedure may have a 15 percent failure rate, they are likely to decide against it. If he tells them the procedure has an 85 percent success rate, they tend to opt for it. If a customer at a grocery store sees some cans of his favorite soup on a shelf, he is likely to put one or two in his cart. If there is a sign that says 'Limit: twelve per customer,' he is likely to put four or five in the cart."[7]

People who have been forced to focus on only the negative attributes of themselves and of life are likely to frame their decisions based on those unrealistic assumptions. This also creates self-defeating and self-destructive behaviors, which then make us feel even worse about ourselves and our life.

Expectations also play a big role in how people respond. Doctors have been doing this with the "placebo effect" for years. If you tell someone a hand cream reduces pain, they will feel less pain even if the lotion is just plain hand lotion. It's also why people firmly believe that brand-name products such as pain relievers work better than generic brands. The fact that they pay more for it sets higher expectations of results in their mind.[8]

If we have the expectation that every time we try something we will fail or get made fun of, we will eventually stop trying new things. As parents we can create either expectations of success or failure for our children just by the way we reference something. Saying, "You are going to do fantastic! I love the way you have the courage to try new things," conveys a completely different message than saying, "I wouldn't get too excited. You've never been very good at stuff like this." Our children tend to live up to or down to the expectations we create for them. Set high expectations. They may not always reach them, but they'll do better than if you set low or no expectations for them. They will also develop higher expectations for themselves.

Misperceptions

Many people from abused situations understandably have misperceptions about life, relationships, and parenting. For example, abused people tend to confuse love with abuse. I know people who (whether they will admit it or not) don't think they deserve to be treated with love and respect. Others continue to stay in or find abusive relationships. They may say they want a healthy relationship, but their actions and decisions speak louder than their words.

Coming from toxic backgrounds, we may have misperceptions about what our role and responsibilities as a parent should look like. Especially when we suddenly find ourself a parent but still feel like a kid inside our head. Until we rec-

A Parent's Responsibilities

- A parent must provide for a child's physical needs.
- A parent must protect a child from physical harm.
- A parent must provide for a child's needs for love, attention, and affection.
- A parent must protect a child from emotional harm.
- A parent must provide moral and ethical guidelines for a child.[9]

ognize these misperceptions, we will continue to perpetuate them to the detriment of ourselves and those we care about. That can be dangerous, as research confirms that parents who were abused themselves have a higher rate of abusing their own children.

Another misperception we might have is that if it wasn't physical abuse, it wasn't really abuse. Abuse takes many different forms. Not recognizing that we were abused only delays our ability to heal from our wounds. When we don't recognize abuse for what it is, we run the risk of exposing our children to that type of abuse. My mother made the comment once that she never abused us because she never hit us to the point of drawing blood (she also maintained that she wasn't an alcoholic because she only drank beer). I'm sure she believed that.

Here are some common misperceptions that people who are at risk of child maltreatment exhibit. See if any of these are familiar:

- *Unrealistic Parental Expectations of the Child*—
  Studies have found that at-risk parents expect and

demand their infants and children behave in a manner that is developmentally inappropriate for their ages. These parents expect more than is reasonable from their children (i.e., expecting a six-month-old to be potty trained). They have expectations of their children that they are incapable of fulfilling. This stems from a lack of knowledge regarding early childhood development and the parents' own childhood experiences.

- *Lack of Empathy*—A second common trait of potentially abusive parents is the inability to be empathically aware of their children's needs. The more in touch one is with their own emotions the more they can recognize the feelings of others. Unfortunately, many abused people have shut down their feelings as a survival mechanism. This causes them to ignore their child's emotional needs.

- *Valuing Physical Punishment*—Potentially abusive parents have a strong belief in the value of physical punishment. These parents believe that babies should not be "given in to," and that children must periodically be shown "who is boss." Much of what abusive parents find wrong with their children reflects the behaviors for which they were criticized and punished as children; therefore, the punishment carries the approval of traditional family authority.[10]

If you have any of the above misperceptions regarding parenting, I urge you to seek the advice of a qualified professional counselor. While these attitudes might seem reasonable and accurate at the time, they are misperceptions that need to be corrected.

Many abused people think they deserved the abuse they were subjected to because they were bad. As awful as that conclusion is, it is less terrifying to a child than believing that their parent is a bad person who does not love them. Let me state this again: YOU are not a bad person. It was not *your* fault you were abused. And you did not deserve to be abused. Remember, if someone harms you, there is something wrong with them, not you. Normal people do not go around destroying other human beings. Okay?

Overcoming Our Fears

One of the biggest fears I had before having children was that I would "ruin" my children. I was especially concerned about having a son, because I knew how easy it would be for me to destroy him. I was hard on myself and could only imagine how hard I could be on a young boy. I waited until I was thirty years old to have my first child, principally because I was still a pretty angry man at that time in my life. I hoped if I waited long enough, I would somehow miraculously "mature" out of my pain and anger. That didn't happen, but it did give me time to get my act together enough to understand some of the reasons why I felt and acted the way I did. It also allowed me to go through some counseling to begin to heal.

I made a lot of mistakes as a dad until I became a Christian when my kids were eight and ten years old. I still made a lot of mistakes after that point, but at least then I was able to recognize them and repent for them. But Christianity did several things for me. It gave me a foundation of information and moral principles to base my decisions upon (not just my own). It gave me time-tested wisdom on everything from marriage, parenting, manhood, and living life successfully. It gave me a heavenly Father who loved me unconditionally, one who forgave me for all my sins. And it introduced me to a healthy group of people to learn from and be mentored by. Was everyone I met in church a good person? No, of course not. Churches are filled with hypocrites and wounded people—just like I was. In ministry work I've been wounded far more by Christians than by non-Christians. But I found a lot more decent people in church than I ever did in bars or nightclubs.

All people fear the same thing—rejection and abandonment. Even people with good childhoods fear this. Everybody wants to be accepted, admired, and loved. But when we have been rejected by our parents (through words or actions), it is especially painful. Fear keeps us from loving others for fear they will reject us. Don't allow your fears to dominate your life. There is no logical reason why your spouse or children will act in the same way your parents did. Different people, different circumstances. Don't allow this misperception—that everyone will betray you the same way your parents did—to keep you from giving love to and accepting love from those who deserve it. You are hurting them and yourself when you operate under that misperception. It takes courage to risk being hurt again, but I'm confident you can do it.

Our fears are the biggest things that hold us back from having a good life. Fear paralyzes us and keeps us from trying new and exciting things. Fear prevents living a life worth living.

Breaking Unhealthy Parental Behaviors

Especially for those of us who have developed either per-fectionistic tendencies or have control issues, parenting can bring out the worst in our ability to parent effectively. Some unhealthy behaviors include helicopter parenting, being overly permissive, or being too strict. The following are some com-mon unhealthy parenting styles.[11] Be aware of tendencies you may have in any of these areas and seek help to remedy them.

Helicopter parents are those who hover over their chil-dren, never allowing them to fail. They micromanage their children's lives, never allowing them to control their own schedule, never allowing them to control their activities and experiences in education, sports, and other facets of life. This does great damage as children do not learn the valuable at-tribute of perseverance. Failing, getting up, and trying again until we succeed is not only the best teacher but also develops healthy self-esteem in children. Children who never fail, fail to learn. By not suffering the consequences of failing, it does not allow them to learn the concept of accountability—a re-quirement to be successful in life. These parents have control issues from their own childhoods.

Karaoke parents are those who do not present clear boundaries and parameters for their children. They are more concerned with being liked than being respected by their children. These children fail to develop a sense of security and a healthy self-esteem. Kids need parents they can respect and look up to, not be friends with. These parents likely suffer from emotional insecurities.

Dry cleaner parents don't provide their children with proper mentoring or face-to-face time. They abdicate their parental responsibilities and fail to bond with their children. These parents are often self-centered or oblivious or feel inadequate to the task of relating to their children.

Volcano parents still have unrealized dreams from their pasts and try to fulfill them through their children. We all know about Little League Dad who tries to relive his glory days through his son. Or Beauty Queen Mom who tries to re-create a dream she gave up on years ago through her daughter. These parents often have baggage from their past that they have not dealt with. As is always the case, kids have a better chance of growing up if their parents do so first.

Dropout parents fail to provide a healthy role model of finishing what they start or to provide the tools their children need. These parents weren't mature enough to have children in the first place and are not ready for that responsibility. Unfortunately, the children of these parents end up not being prepared to launch into the world.

Bullied parents lack the courage and strength to lead strong-willed children. Their children are leaderless, as their personalities are stronger than their parents'. These parents lack the backbone to "choose their battles" and not be subservient to their children.

Groupie parents fail to realize their children need leaders, not servants. They lavish too much time and attention on their children, never denying them anything. This can increase the child's self-esteem to unhealthy levels. These parents need to recognize that loving your children means treating them as people, not idols. They need to learn when to say no and help their children understand that they are not the center of the universe. Otherwise they run the risk of creating narcissistic children.

Commando parents are focused on attaining compliance and perfection in their children. Their kids live in anxiety, frustration, and exhaustion trying to meet these militant expectations. These parents feel their own reputations are reflected in their children's performance.

Finally, *survivor parents* are parents from abusive backgrounds who can often re-create the dysfunction by going too far toward the opposite end of the spectrum and spoiling or overindulging their children. This is usually done in an attempt to put as much distance as possible between their children and abuse. However, abuse lies at both ends of that spectrum.

If you recognize any of those patterns in your parenting style, I encourage you to attend some parenting classes, read books, and find support groups to help you understand the process taking place. The good thing about parenting is that it's never too late to become a better parent.

What Children Need and Why

One of the best things we can do to raise our children successfully is to establish nurturing routines. The predictability of a daily routine helps children understand that the world is a safe place where they can learn and grow without fear. Since that is something that most people who were abused lacked, let's look at some ways to implement these things in your children's lives.

One thing children need in their lives is security. Security is imperative for children to feel safe and thrive. This means meeting their needs for shelter, food, clothing, medical care,

How to Help Your Kids Thrive

- Meet their everyday needs (food, safety, nurturing, etc.).
- Provide safety and security.
- Give love and hugs (cuddling, hugs, kisses, etc.).
- Shower them with praise.
- Smile at them.
- Talk to them (a lot).
- Listen to them.
- Teach them new things.
- Nurture their feelings.
- Reward them (positive reinforcement).[12]

and protection from harm. Kids need to know they can count on their parents. Being dependable and creating a consistent home life is hugely powerful in growing healthy children.

Stability is also important. Stability consists of a stable household and extended family without a lot of chaos. Being part of a larger community also ensures a sense of belonging. Try to minimize disruptions in their lives if things like divorce, job loss, or illness occur.

The parental care a child receives makes a big difference in the lives they lead. For instance, just by observing the quality of care a child receives at 42 months, researchers can predict with a 77 percent accuracy rate which children will drop out of high school.[13]

Make sure your children get the best possible education for their future. This includes schooling but also invaluable life lessons by spending quality time together with parents. People I have spoken to who have overcome abuse and poverty rated education as the most important factor in their success.

Structure is essential for children. Rules, boundaries, and limitations give them a sense of security. Without them children are forced to grow up too fast and lose respect for the adults in their life. Kids without boundaries (even small children) often act out in an effort to find out where the boundaries are.

And of course, what children need most is just to be loved. Loved unconditionally if possible, but just plain loved regardless. Love covers a multitude of mistakes that we make as a parent. Our kids don't expect us to be perfect, but they do expect that we will try our best and not give up.

7

Good Kids, Bad Kids

> When a child hits an adult we call it hostility. When an adult hits an adult, we call it assault. When an adult hits a child, we call it discipline.
>
> —Haim G. Ginott

Many parents, especially those from dysfunctional homes, tend to feel that the choices their kids make are a reflection upon them. If their child ends up going to an Ivy League college, gets a good job, marries well, and has beautiful, well-behaved children, we feel great about the job we did as parents. But if they dropped out of school, got hooked on drugs, and can't hold a job, we think of ourselves as failures as a parent. And certainly, to some degree the way we parent does influence the choices our children make. But it's important to remember that just like God gave each of us free will, he also gave our children free will. That means that they can each make their own choices, regardless of how they were parented. It's why great parents have kids who rebel and make bad choices, and why horrible parents can have kids who turn out fantastic. Their bad choices are not necessarily a reflection upon you any more than your poor choices are a negative reflection upon God. That said, if we are not going to take credit for the bad choices our kids make, perhaps we shouldn't be so quick to take credit when they make good choices either.

One of the challenges that people from abusive upbringings struggle with is understanding healthy ways to discipline their children. Since we tend to imitate what was modeled for us as children by our caregivers, this presents problems for parents in these situations, especially if one has not healed from those childhood wounds. Behavior modification is one of the more important aspects of parenting. Done right, it helps raise healthy, happy, and successful people. Done wrong, it can cause many problems during childhood and later on down the road.

Here are some perspectives about disciplining your children that I found helpful in changing the paradigms that I was taught as a child.

Discipline vs. Punishment

Like a lot of people of my age group, I was raised in a home that used a good amount of corporal punishment to program us to not do things we weren't supposed to do. The problem with physical punishment is that, by its very nature, it is performed most often when the parent is angry, which is never a good time to teach a child a lesson. Corporal punishment not only hurts the child, but it hurts the parent and the parent/child relationship as well. I've come to recognize that discipline and not punishment is a better way to parent our children.

I'll also admit that I've changed my attitude on this subject over the years. As a younger father, I believed that since my parents used it and I turned out okay, then it must be okay for my kids. Not that our kids were subject to many spankings (at least not as many as they think they were), but I wasn't in the camp of those who think that "any spanking is child abuse." Here's why I changed my opinion on this controversial subject.

I believe all of us want to raise healthy children. One of the ways we do that is to teach them ways to live a successful life. Teaching them to be considerate of others, compassionate, well-behaved, and respectful are just some of the traits they need to learn. Unfortunately children often resist learning these traits and so have to be encouraged. We can "encourage" them by either disciplining or punishing them.

The goal of discipline is to teach, not to punish. While punishment is often done in anger, we seldom discipline in anger. Punishment is something you do *to* a child; discipline is what you do *for* a child. Discipline uses logic and a considered plan to teach a lesson. Punishment's nature is to inflict pain in order to make a little person want to avoid that consequence of the behavior in the future. That's not to say that a swat on the butt when a small child is doing something life-threateningly dangerous won't be remembered and the behavior avoided in the future—just like if you mouth off to a bully and get popped in the nose, you're not likely to try

Differences between Discipline and Punishment

While discipline and punishment might have similar goals (managing and improving a child's behavior), they are vastly different in their approach and the impression left on a child.

Discipline	Punishment
Used before, during, and after an event	Used only after an event
Teaches	Enforces
Based on the child's development and ability to change	Denies child's ability to change
Respects child	Disrespects child
Educates child	Inflicts pain on child
Teaches internal self-control	Managed by external control
Builds trust	Builds resentment
Anger to remorse	Anger to revenge
Increases child's self-esteem	Decreases child's self-esteem
Parent feels satisfaction	Parent feels guilty (maybe)

that again real soon. And of course toddlers can be extremely defiant. As a dad, I always thought they should learn quickly that while the Lion (me) was good, he was also a bit dangerous to disrespect. But in general, a better way to discipline kids is to use the situation as a teaching lesson and not an opportunity to inflict pain.[1]

I recently watched a video on YouTube of a Middle Eastern man beating his adult male slave with a belt. It was brutal to watch and made me sick to my stomach. But it was not all that much different from what I remember from my experiences as a child being spanked with a belt. Perhaps if each of us were forced to watch ourselves spanking our children, we would find other ways to discipline them.

We often hear the adage "Spare the rod, spoil the child" used when referring to correcting children. That's generally taken to mean if you don't use the rod on them, they will end up being spoiled brats. And kids who are not subject to healthy discipline do tend to become insufferable little monsters. But when that passage was written, a "rod" was used as a tool by shepherds for *guiding* their sheep (or even rescuing them), not inflicting pain upon them.

Additionally, the portion of the brain (prefrontal cortex) that controls decision making and impulse control doesn't fully develop in human beings until they are in their late twenties. Therefore punishment may be counterproductive in that they may sometimes make bad decisions even if they don't intend to. But by using positive discipline techniques, your children will automatically learn to follow them, regardless of their level of brain development. Positive rewards are a much more powerful learning and motivating device than are negative or hurtful consequences. While fear of punishment may be a motivating emotion, it only works until the child gets bigger than the parent. Healthy discipline teaches lessons that last a lifetime.

Using Discipline

But that doesn't mean that children do not need guidelines, limits, and boundaries. In fact, children need limits—they're essential to healthy maturity. A 1967 study by Stanley Coopersmith showed that the parents who gave their kids the most rules and limitations had children with the highest self-esteem, while those who gave their children the most freedoms had kids with the lowest self-esteem.[2] So how do we use discipline (as opposed to punishment) to help set healthy limits for our children?

First, understand that if you use discipline consistently when your children are young (toddlers), it makes disciplining them later much easier. Be sure they clearly understand the rules of your home. At this stage you have to provide a lot of guidance, training them all the time. Teaching children to listen to and obey you when they are little allows you to relax the rules as they get older. But this takes a lot of work when they are young.

All forms of discipline have common components that should be followed:

1. Be consistent and fair. Consistency is important in establishing trust and helping your child understand your expectations. If you change the rules all the time, you can't expect him to know what they are.
2. Use appropriate consequences for each offense.
3. Present a united front with your spouse.
4. Give more praise than correction. Avoid long lectures.
5. Tailor discipline to fit the child's bent.
6. Know the developmental phases that your children go through at different ages.

When you are contemplating disciplining a child for their behavior, take into consideration a few factors to determine how severe the discipline should be:

- Is this behavior typical or part of normal childhood development? A two-year-old is going to act like a two-year-old from time to time, no matter how well the child normally behaves.

- Does the behavior occur at any specific time or occasion? If a child only starts misbehaving or has a bad attitude right before dinner, perhaps there are issues like blood sugar levels or other factors involved.

- Consider questions like, *Why would a child act this way? Is this typical behavior of other children or specific to your child? Is the behavior dangerous, destructive, or illegal?* (Certainly any of these three would warrant a stronger response than a minor infraction of family rules.) *What are the long-range consequences of this behavior?* Considering those things might give you an idea on how important it is to intervene.

- Lastly, stay calm and pick your battles. Not everything is worthy of an all-out war. If you fight all the battles, you will eventually lose the war.

One strategy that works well in modifying children's behavior is to allow them to participate in designing their consequences. That sounds counterintuitive but works surprisingly well. While setting up or discussing a family value, get your child's input on what the consequences should be if he misbehaves. If you haven't already developed a consequence, you can ask your children what they think is a fair and reasonable idea. That's not to say you don't determine the consequence as a parent, but this at least helps children take ownership of and buy into the program. Without that buy-in, children feel like they have no control over their circumstances, and all of us want control over our lives.

Healthy discipline should also have several goals in mind. The first is to build trust between the parent and the child. Trust is the foundation of all human relationships. Lack of trust in a person inhibits their ability to develop a conscience. Once you discipline your child, don't hold a grudge. The slate is wiped clean and you are starting over—sort of like how God forgives us when we sin and ask for forgiveness. He doesn't hold it against us but forgets all about it.

The second goal is to build self-esteem in the child. If we punish kids too often, they begin to believe themselves unworthy and *unable* to be good. As dads, we need to change the belief behind the behavior, not just the behavior. If our children believe they are not capable of being a good person, it doesn't matter how much we discipline them; they still will not be able to change that perception—any change will only be temporary. Our kids' perception of themselves is the key to their attitude, motivation, and behavior. If they believe themselves capable of something, they will be. If they believe they can't do something, they won't even try. Even though all people have value, those who believe they are worthless tend to act as if they are worthless.

Next is to teach new behaviors. Just as we adults don't know what we don't know, neither do our children. A child who has never been exposed to a situation or doesn't know (or is too young to know) the rules of a new circumstance cannot be expected to know how to act or what the boundaries are. Part of a parent's job is to teach our children how to live life successfully. The best time to learn things is when we make mistakes. It's also important to understand that we learn in stages— knowledge is accumulative. We build on understanding something by adding to what we've previously learned. So often we have to repeat mistakes in order to learn the entire lesson. Using punishment short-circuits that process.

Discipline also allows parents to reteach existing negative behaviors. That's why it's never too late to change the way you relate to your children. Even teenagers with established bad habits or behaviors can be "reprogrammed" through consistent discipline.

Lastly, discipline (as opposed to punishment, in which they have no control) helps a child gain self-control. It teaches them how to think for themselves and how to act in the future when faced with similar situations. They must learn how to manage and control themselves. We can't be with our kids twenty-four hours a day, but we want them to hear our voice whispering in their ear when faced with circumstances that could be troublesome or potentially dangerous for them.

The Three Rs of Punishment

1. *Resentment*: "This is unfair. I can't trust adults."
2. *Revenge*: "They are winning now, but I'll get even."
3. *Retreat*, in one of three extremes:
   a. *Rebellion*: "I'll do what I want and just be more careful not to get caught next time. I have a right to lie and cheat under these circumstances."

b. *Reduced self-esteem*: "I must really be a bad person who deserves to be punished. I will keep trying to please, but I'm not much good at it."

c. *Retirement*: "I give up. I can't win, so why try? I wish people would just leave me alone."[3]

Also remember that consequences should be used for both negative *and* positive situations (good consequences for positive situations and bad consequences for negative situations). Remember to reward the behaviors you like just as you discipline the ones you want to correct.

Always follow through with whatever consequences you set for violating your family rules. If you don't follow through (every single time), everything you do or say will be ignored. We've all seen the parent who keeps repeating, "This is the last time!" or who continues to count to three over and over again. These parents have children who are in control of the relationship.

If you do follow through with consequences, it usually only takes a couple of times for children to stop testing the limits of their boundaries. This works no matter how old they are—again, it's never too late to change behaviors (in us or them). Mostly we want to remember that discipline while parenting requires us to use firmness, dignity, and respect when exercising our authority.

You can't force your children to obey you. Well, maybe you can—for a while anyway, when they are little. But eventually they will rebel and disobey you, if for no other reason than they can. Also, children can be compliant on the outside and still be disobedient on the inside. That's one reason why screaming, yelling, threatening, and repeating yourself are such ineffective strategies.

When your children become eighteen years old, you probably won't be around all the time to yell at them and force them to make the right decision. A big-picture vision of raising children is to tell them what you expect from them, what the benefits are if they obey, and what the consequences are if they don't. Then let them choose. Of course that requires you to be very diligent in making sure you follow through with said consequences (both positive and negative). But the goal is to teach them how to make decisions and to know that each decision has consequences. That's a much better way to approach life successfully—especially when they move out of the house and out from under your protection and guidance.

Some of you may have children who are more challenging than others. They may not be able to learn things easily, may struggle in school, and may generally seem unruly or hyperactive and unable to focus. Before allowing the school (or anyone else) to label them as having attention deficit disorder (ADD) or attention deficit hyperactivity disorder (ADHD), you should consider a few things. First, children develop at differing rates and schedules (boys are usually a few years behind girls until at least adolescence). Additionally, the education format used in public schools is generally not conducive to the way most boys learn best. Boys typically struggle with sitting quietly for long periods of time while being lectured to (I still do, and to my knowledge I don't have ADD). Recesses and PE are being cut back, which especially harms boys, who need that release of pent-up energy.

Diagnosing ADHD with any degree of certainty is difficult—primarily because the symptoms (distractibility, impulsivity, and hyperactivity) are consistent with normal behavior in all young children. The challenge is really this: Is the child exhibiting *more* of any of those traits than he should be for his age? Since nearly all preschoolers exhibit these symptoms, a child shouldn't be diagnosed before the age of seven. ADHD-like symptoms such as distractibility or hyperactivity can also be caused by a variety of other conditions, including sleep disorders, anxiety, or even cultural differences.[4]

In addition, we need to be aware of the distinction between ADD and a child being distractible. Kids with ADD pay attention to nothing. Kids that are distractible pay attention to everything.

Also, if your child has been traumatized (which could be anything from having been through a family divorce to having been physically injured in some way), he or she may suffer from some form of post-traumatic stress disorder (PTSD). PTSD and ADHD have similar symptoms in educational environments, especially in boys. Yet they are very different issues—one is a physical reaction to a traumatic event and the other is a chemical imbalance. Unfortunately many children with PTSD are misdiagnosed with ADHD and given a stimulant such as Ritalin, which only exacerbates the problem. PTSD is an anxiety disorder (not a concentration issue) and is treated with anti-anxiety medication, pretty much the exact opposite of a stimulant. You can see how that might cause problems.

I am not saying ADD and ADHD are not legitimate diagnoses in some children, but I think too many children today (especially boys) are medicated for just being boys or for being naturally rambunctious.

Wise parents make sure their children are protected from unnecessary and inaccurate labeling, medical procedures, and medications.

Boundaries

All children need boundaries. They need clear-cut rules, structure, and guidelines. They thrive under firm supervision and guidance. We provide those things to our children by using discipline.

Discipline comes in two forms—internal and external. Internal discipline or self-discipline is what we strive to teach our children by applying external discipline. External discipline is applied in a variety of forms—allowing them to suffer the consequences of their actions, teaching them the pleasures of delayed gratification, understanding the relationship between hard work and success, and developing personal accountability. Kids who are not subjected to healthy discipline while growing up tend to live unhappy lives and create chaos in the lives of those around them. When we discipline our children, we are actually preparing them for much more fulfilling lives.

We teach boundaries and self-discipline by using consequences and accountability. We allow them to suffer the consequences of their choices and decisions. That can be difficult enough for parents who do not carry around a legacy of pain. It's even more trying for a parent who was wounded in childhood to allow his child to suffer at all.

Without accountability in our lives, we tend to make our own rules and codes of conduct. Children from an early age need to learn that their actions have positive or negative consequences. And they need to learn that their decisions don't affect just them, but others as well. Unfortunately, holding our children accountable and allowing them to realize the consequences of their decisions forces them to suffer.

But suffering and overcoming challenges is a key component in creating powerful character qualities in males and females alike. Life is difficult, and it doesn't seem to care about our needs or wants most of the time. Also, it never seems to get any easier no matter how much older and experienced we get. Life still presents challenges. The good part is that those challenges are what develop our character and teach us to be the kind of people who can make a difference in the world.

Greatness is not possible without some sort of failure to overcome. Suffering develops character. Without suffering, we never have the opportunity to test ourselves and see what we are made of.

If that's true, then it goes without saying that our children need to suffer in order to develop a healthy character. For so many of us, the challenge is, how do we allow our children to suffer enough to develop character without traumatizing them? Many parents today "rescue" their kids too often, never allowing them to face the consequences of any of the choices they make. Helicopter parents hover over their children, never allowing them to take healthy risks and possibly get hurt. Since it's virtually impossible to succeed at life without taking some risks, these children are psychologically crippled by the very thing their parents think is helping them.

Suffering teaches character, and yet for most parents, it is unthinkable that they should allow their children to experience any form of suffering. Many of us reading this book have suffered in childhood, and our greatest desire is to ensure that our children never have to suffer like we did. But many young people today have never suffered a day in their lives, and so some (even those from the best families) feel lost, unnecessary, or insignificant. This can create a host of problems for a young person.

Persevering through our struggles matures us and develops healthy self-esteem. It helps us feel valuable and important. Children need to struggle, if for no other reason than that. They need to wrestle with questions and problems. It gives them self-confidence and self-esteem to struggle with issues until they solve them. They don't need to be rescued and seldom want to be told all the answers. But they do want to be valued.

Teach your children to learn how to suffer—to suffer "well." Suffering is a fact of life—no one escapes this world without suffering. Those who use that suffering to learn and grow from are much healthier and happier than those who wallow in their despair.

Boundaries are a good way to allow our children to "suffer" under our protective environment. We can teach them and guide them while still allowing them to develop the character necessary to succeed in life.

Environment vs. Genetics

One area that we tend to overlook in the development of our children is the importance of genetic influences, especially when compared to the environmental influences in the lives of our children. I'm not a particularly big proponent of promoting either the nurture or nature theory exclusively in human development. I think most of us are a combination of both our genetic makeup and the environment we were raised in.

Recently, however, I have become more aware of the powerful influence our genetic code plays in our personal development. One rather humorous example of this is the similarities between my biological father and me. I first met him when I was twenty-four years old, a fully developed adult human being. Besides looking alike and standing with the same posture, our wives have delighted over the years in the fact that we also have a predisposition for the same clothing, foods, sleeping style, and a plethora of other habits and behaviors. One day my dad and his wife drove up from California to visit us. He and I showed up wearing the same brown velour shirt (there were probably only two of them in the entire country). According to our wives, even our personal hygiene habits are eerily similar. Clearly, as I was never influenced by him as a child, these idiosyncrasies are the result of genetic coding that somehow determines my unconscious behavior, choices, and preferences in life.

But I have noticed destructive behaviors attributed to some form of genetic imprint. Most of us are aware of the generational cycles (or sins) that occur in families and are passed down from generation to generation. Oftentimes these occur from modeled behaviors, but I'm convinced many are also derived (or at least influenced) from our genetic makeup. Modeled behaviors, especially from primary caretakers, *are* a hugely powerful indicator in our own behavioral outcomes.

Because of modeled behaviors, we often see families where alcoholism, abandonment, or abusive behavior that was modeled by parents is emulated and passed down from one generation to the next. However, genetics also appears to play a significant role in our outcomes, especially if we are unaware of their influence.

I have observed this in many of those we work with in our ministry. For example, virtually every female in every generation of one young woman's family—for as far back as anyone can remember—has been an unwed teenage mother. Even females who had been adopted out of the biological family followed this genetic blueprint for their lives. Knowing this predilection, this young woman's mother and father were determined to break this "cycle" with their daughter. However, despite raising her in a relatively healthy two-parent environment, being aware of the challenges they faced, and talking with her about those challenges, it took all of their mightiest efforts to keep that genetic legacy from coming to fruition. It was almost as if she was predisposed to make choices that compelled her to accomplish the genetic coding in her DNA. She was prone to make self-destructive decisions (and have attitudes) that reflected those of the women in her heritage, despite not being exposed to the behavior modeled in her family of origin. Thankfully she is now twenty years old so will never be a *teenage* mother and hopefully will never be an *unwed* mother either. But the challenges were and still are formidable in helping her break the cycle that was engrained in her DNA throughout generations of her lineage.

This phenomenon is also observed in adopted children who act out in behaviors (substance abuse, promiscuity, out-of-wedlock childbirth) similar to their birth parents even though never having met them. Certainly there are other factors involved in the behaviors of adopted children, not the least of which involve issues of abandonment, but many children raised in healthy adoptive families make destructive life choices eerily similar to those that their birth parents engaged in, even though they may not have any awareness of those behaviors.

I believe wholeheartedly that the models we are raised with while growing up are the biggest influences in the way we learn to live our lives. But perhaps more often than we recognize, we are preprogrammed or predisposed to make choices that result in outcomes that have a basis in our generational heritage. Being conscious of these historical "tendencies" allows us to make intentional choices to break those generational influences instead of inadvertently falling into a preordained future.

As an example, if the women in your heritage have had problems with addictions or alcoholism, there is a greater likelihood of your daughter having a predisposition to be attracted to these substances. If the males have been alcoholics or criminals, your son might have a bent toward those behaviors. I understand that the medical profession considers alcoholism a "disease." Whether it is a disease or whether it's a choice (which I believe) is up for debate. Regardless, there appears to be a genetic component involved.

Additionally, there is new scientific research which expounds that various factors such as how much your father drank or your grandmother smoked may have altered your genes and can be passed along to your children. *Epigenetics* is the research on how our diets, the toxins we are exposed to, and our stress levels at work may be subtly altering the genetic legacy we pass on to our children. This research posits that the new "epidemics" of autoimmune disorders, obesity, autism, and diabetes may be traced back to the chemicals our grandparents were exposed to. We see the flip side of this today when pregnant women are encouraged to take folic acid and vitamin B-12, as these decrease the risk of asthma, and brain and spinal cord defects in fetuses.[5] That said, even the traumas we are exposed to as children, which alter the neural pathways in our brains, are a factor in altering our gene pool. A group of behavioral geneticists in Switzerland have determined that early psychological trauma may cause lasting changes in the brain that promote aggressive behavior, depression, and anxiety in adulthood. This indicates that social learning may not be the only cause of these behaviors in abused children.[6]

Education is the first step to breaking generational cycles. Being aware of your lineage and making your children aware of their genetic propensities can go a long way to helping them avoid those traps. It also helps *you* not get blindsided by some tragedy that comes out of the blue. Other things like mental illnesses, diseases, depression, and eating disorders also have genetic components associated with them and are treatable with counseling and medication.

Look at your heritage and your spouse's heritage closely. See if there are specific cycles that present themselves throughout generations that need to be addressed. Many people are caught off guard by not being aware of potential potholes in the genetic coding passed on to their children (or to themselves). It's not that your children are predestined to act this way; it just may be something you need to be aware of in order to develop a comprehensive plan to raise them into healthy adulthood.

8

Healthy Relationship Practices

> With everything that has happened to you, you can either
> feel sorry for yourself, or treat what has happened as a gift.
> Everything is either an opportunity to grow, or an obstacle
> to keep you from growing. You get to choose.
>
> —Dr. Wayne Dyer

Another challenge people from toxic or broken homes face is
knowing what a healthy relationship looks like. I remember
when my wife and I were first married, I had a lot of strange
(in hindsight) views about what a marriage relationship and
parenting looked like. My wife would object and say, "But
that's just not normal!" In my naive confidence, I would respond, "Yes, it is. That's the way we always did it in my house
growing up." Of course, it wasn't "normal" behavior. It was
the twisted behavior that was modeled for me while I was
growing up.

We all enter relationships with conscious and unconscious expectations that we have derived from our experiences and the world around us. When we come from dysfunctional homes, those expectations are often damaging to us and to others. Those expectations also impact the way we parent our children.

Our ministry hosts a single mom family camp almost every summer. We invite single moms and their kids to a free three-day weekend camp. We provide male mentors to play with the kids all weekend, and we provide workshops, mentoring, and time for relaxation for the moms. The first year we hosted a camp, the feedback from the moms stunned us. Many of them said things like, "The best thing we got from the camp was watching the married couples who volunteered interact at lunch and dinner. Our kids never get to see healthy couples talking, disagreeing, and solving problems." We now include as many married couple volunteers as possible.

We talked about mentoring earlier, so let's talk now about the important aspects of relationships. Find some healthy families to observe if you need a model.

Best Parenting Advice Ever? Love Your Spouse

Several different people are credited with the quote "The greatest gift a man can give his children is to love their mother." I would say it applies to women just as much. Loving our spouse compensates for a lot of mistakes we make as a parent. I believe it is the most important thing we can strive for as parents. Kids whose parents love each other are more secure and confident in their roles in life. They are less likely to divorce or become unwed parents.

It is truly a gift when we teach our children the healthy way a man and woman love and respect one another, and how a married couple models their masculine and feminine roles as husband and wife. Just as fathers are the biggest influences as role models regarding masculinity for their sons, so too are mothers the greatest role models of femininity for their daughters. A mother teaches her what a woman's roles in life are, how to fulfill those roles, and what healthy femininity looks like. A mother also models to her daughter how to love a man, what level of respect men deserve, and what a woman's role is in marriage. A happy, secure, and confident wife teaches her daughters good things about men and relationships.

A father teaches sons and daughters how a man loves a woman and how a woman should be cherished. How a man speaks to his wife is a powerful lesson to their children. It teaches boys how they are supposed to treat a woman and what level of respect she deserves. Tell your wife in front of your daughter every day that you love her and spend time praising her for her good attributes. Tell her you appreciate her when she does something for you. Don't just comment when she disappoints you. Look for opportunities to use the power God has given you to lift her up to be the maximum woman God intended her to be. When your daughter sees those actions modeled, she will internalize them as how a woman should be treated. That way she won't marry a guy who berates and disrespects her (hopefully).

Married people are also healthier, happier, and better off financially than their single counterparts. Having a spouse means you have someone to rely on to help shoulder the burdens of life and raising a family. Despite the fact that many people recite the mantra that marriage is good for men and bad for women, research clearly shows that marriage is healthy for both sexes, and the vast majority of women prosper by being in a marriage. Married people are physically and emotionally healthier and live longer than their single counterparts. Married men and women both report less depression and anxiety, and lower levels of other types of psychological stress. Single people have much higher mortality rates (50 percent higher for women and 250 percent higher for men) than married people. Women tend to live longer when married because they have more money and live in better neighborhoods with adequate health care (statistics show that just over half of single women have health insurance, while 83 percent of married women do). Married men tend to live longer because they stop risky behaviors such as drinking, drugs, driving fast (while intoxicated), and putting themselves in a variety of dangerous situations. Married men also eat much better diets and have wives who monitor their health and force them to see the doctor when necessary.[1]

Your spouse is also your greatest asset as a parent. A wife can build her husband up in front of the children, edifying him and gaining him respect that he couldn't garner on his own. When she shows him respect and actively acknowledges his leadership, you can bet your children will as well. But if she is contemptible toward you, your children will probably not have much respect for you. She can also keep you up to speed on the emotional challenges your kids are facing. Lastly, she is an excellent barometer to help you gauge how well you are doing as a father.

A husband can ensure that his wife is respected by their children. Dad is often viewed as the rule enforcer in the family. He typically possesses an innate "fear factor" in his children that allows him to make sure things run smoothly. You'll notice that when Dad is gone for long periods or emotionally absent, chaos often reigns in the household. Self-discipline lags and open rebellion is more prevalent. Especially as children become teenagers, they have a tendency to attempt to rebel against Mom's authority. Dad can ease that transition by keeping sons in line and by interceding in mother-daughter conflicts before they get too out of control.

Of course, not all families operate in that format. The traditional nuclear family structure is not so much the norm anymore. Single moms frequently lead their families with authority, and sometimes Mom is the rule enforcer in the family even if Dad is present. But a father's position designed by God as the leader of his home gives him a certain authority. He frequently does not have to initially earn that authority, but he can only maintain it by earning it.

But beyond all that, your marriage is important, especially for your kids. Children need both the complementary parenting styles of a mother (nurturing) and a father (authoritative) in order to thrive. These love styles (performance-based and unconditional) help teach children character traits and life lessons they need in order to be successful human beings. One of the biggest myths of our culture is that divorce is the best thing for children when a marriage becomes unhappy—that staying married "for the kids' sake" is a mistake.

A wide range of research shows that children from single-parent homes fare more poorly than their counterparts from two-parent families in virtually every measurable outcome. Unfortunately, according to vital-statistics data from the Centers for Disease Control and Prevention, 41 percent of all births are now a result of nonmarital child-bearing (much higher in minority homes).[2] Just a few examples of how children fare more poorly in these situations include:

- Children in father-absent homes are five times more likely to be poor and ten times as likely to be extremely poor than children living with a mother and a father.
- Children from single-parent homes are much more likely to be neglected, and sexually, psychologically, and emotionally abused than their two-parent counterparts.
- Teenagers from single-parent homes were one and a half to two times more at risk for illegal drug use than teens from intact homes.
- Boys fourteen to twenty-two years of age who grow up outside intact families are twice as likely to end up in jail. Every year a boy spends living without a father increases the odds of future incarceration by 5 percent. A boy born to an unwed mother is two and a half times more likely to end up in prison than boys raised in two-parent homes.
- Separation or frequent transitions (divorce, new partners, etc.) increase a girl's risk of early menarche, sexual activity, and pregnancy. Women whose parents separated early in life experience twice the risk of early menstruation, more than four times the risk

of early sexual intercourse, and two and a half times higher risk of early pregnancy compared to women in intact families. The longer a woman lived with both parents, the lower her risk of early reproductive development.

- On average, educational achievement in children from one-parent homes is significantly lower. Children from single-parent homes score lower on tests and have lower grade-point averages than those from two-parent, biological families. Children from one-parent homes are more than twice as likely to drop out of school as children from two-parent homes. Additionally, nearly all educational outcomes (grade-point average, test scores, achievement test scores, and high school/college graduation) are, on average, lower in students from single-parent homes than students from intact families.[3]

It's human nature to spend our most precious commodity—our time—on the things we value most. If we want to be better parents, we need to focus our time and energy on our marriages. We need to have "marriage-focused" marriages instead of "children-focused" marriages. It's important for parents to remember that your marriage will be around long after your kids are gone. And it's worth staying together for the long run. Even though our kids are grown and gone (most of the time), I'd be lost without my wife. She knows me better than anyone in the world. She cares about me more than anyone else in the world. She appreciates me better than anyone else could. Building that kind of relationship takes time. It isn't done overnight or even over years. It takes decades.

So, how do you divorce proof your marriage? How do you keep intimacy alive in your relationship? There's one simple, foolproof method. Pray together daily. It's that simple. Simple, but not so easy. Perhaps because it is so powerful a tool, it is difficult to get started and easy to stop doing. Once you stop, it is even more difficult to get going again. But I guarantee you, there is nothing you can do that will bring you and your spouse closer together than to pray together every day. Men, I'm not sure why, but it has been my experience, and every guy I've talked to confirms it, that if the husband does not initiate this action, it probably won't happen. Maybe it's part of our leadership role in the home that makes it necessary for us to initiate this action.

Commitment—the Most Important Trait

Almost any adult can perform the physical act that creates a child. But that doesn't make them a father or mother. Being a good parent takes commitment. It's why a dedicated stepparent or foster parent can be a better mom or dad than an uninvolved biological mother or father.

Commitment is keeping the promises we've made, including implicit promises, such as when we commit to being a parent by simply becoming one. It is our duty to raise our children to the best of our abilities. The word *duty* conveys a moral commitment to someone or something. That moral commitment results in an action, not just a passive feeling or recognition. Being committed to our children means that not only will we stay, we will do everything in our power to heal ourselves so that we can be the best parents possible.

Men, would you die for your wife and children? I would, and I think most men would be willing to sacrifice themselves for the sake of their family. But have you told your wife and children that you'd die for them? That's very powerful—to know that someone cares enough for you to die for you. I'd feel honored to know someone would die for me.

I encourage you to confess that to your family. They need to know.

Parental commitment (especially by fathers) is rated as the number one factor in developing self-esteem in children. I remember when our children were young, whenever my wife and I would have an argument or disagreement, they would run and hide. When I asked them why, they said they were scared. They weren't scared because our arguments were violent or even particularly loud. They said they were scared because so many of their friends at school had parents who divorced. They were afraid that we would get divorced. I had to assure them (many times) that I was committed to always being married to their mother and that we would never get a divorce. That I would always be their father, I would never leave them, and I would always love them, no matter what. They needed assurances of my commitment in order to feel safe and secure.

Our ministry works with so many kids whose fathers (or mothers) have not made that commitment. These kids are most often scared, insecure, and lost. And kids in the foster care system have lost the commitment of both of their parents. It's a sad and tragic fate for these poor children.

Preventing Your Kids from Being Molested

We need to set healthy boundaries for our children as well as for parents, relatives, and strangers. I am always stunned at the number of people who have been molested by a family member and then allow that person unsupervised access to their children. Sex abusers never stop their behavior until they are caught and punished. You also have an obligation to tell others in the family what this person has done. Many won't believe you or will resent your saying something, but you have a responsibility to protect other children from the same thing happening to them that happened to you.

Sex offenders work just as hard at deceiving adults as they do at seducing and silencing children. They are often people we trust and our children love. Their tactics work so well that fewer than 5 percent are reported and successfully prosecuted.[4]

We must talk to our children about this subject. Show of hands—how many of you look forward to having this talk with your children? Me neither. I hated (and resented) the fact that I had to sully my children's innocence in order to protect them from the evil in the world. But if we don't talk to them, who will? Not only that, but this is an ongoing conversation, not a onetime event. We have to give our children the knowledge and information to protect themselves when we are not around. We need to talk to them about sexual abuse and offender behavior. Frankly, it's not our children's job to protect themselves, it's ours.

Sex offenders are very manipulative and are excellent liars. They are clever and adept at gaining the trust and friendship of your child. They confuse the child, make them feel

Advice from Child Molesters

- I am someone you know, but don't really know.
- Talk to your children—prepare them about sex offenders.
- I will make it hard for your child to tell you what I'm doing. Make it easier for them—communicate, listen, believe them.
- Trust your child, not me. They deserve your trust, I don't.
- Teach them about sexuality, private parts, and "secret touching."
- Tell them it's never okay for someone to touch them or ask to be touched.
- Tell them it's always the bigger person's fault and they will not get in trouble.
- Tell your child if they can't tell you, to tell another adult.
- Trust your instincts.[5]

responsible for what's happening, and make them distrust their parents. They make the child believe that they will get in trouble or will be taken away and placed in foster care, never to see their parents again, if they tell. Children are no match for sex offenders.[6]

If your child tells you they have been inappropriately touched or propositioned, believe them. Children seldom make this kind of stuff up (only 1 to 2 percent of reports are falsified). They do not have the knowledge or imagination. Kids lie to get *out* of trouble, not into trouble. Remember, sex offenders are adept at gaining the trust of adults as well. They like to prey upon a single mom's fears about her child's lack of a father figure. But even when children do tell, 52 percent of sex offenders surveyed reported that they were able to "talk the adults out of calling the police."[7] That is unacceptable. These people do not stop offending. You have the duty to protect other children by reporting these violations to the police, even if the offender is your close relative.

Healthy Communication

Words matter. People from abusive situations tend to believe the terrible things that were said to them. This contributes to their own negative self-talk. Unfortunately, our negative self-talk often comes out of our mouth and gets spoken to other little ears, who believe it about themselves. Healthy people believe the nurturing things their parents spoke into their hearts, and they tend to believe good things about themselves even when they end up in difficult circumstances.

As we've talked about earlier, a parent's words have great power over their children. They'll remember many of your comments for years to come—things you don't even remember saying. Their whole outlook on life could be shaped—for better or for worse—by something you say. Whenever possible, use words intentionally to bless and to build up—whether you shout them, whisper them, or simply speak them as a normal part of the day.

One of the chief predictors of a young person's success is their perception of their parents' image of them. Speak encouragement and it builds your children up, empowering them for life. Speak negative words and it cripples the soul of your children. Unfortunately, most of us don't think about what we say before it comes out of our mouth. Especially when upset, we just blow off steam. Oftentimes we don't even mean what we say when we are angry. But our children believe that their all-wise and powerful parents always speak the truth.

Sometimes what we don't say speaks as loud as what we do say. My wife texted me recently and encouraged me to hug our adult daughter and speak some words of love and encouragement to her. She said she has been watching our daughter listen to me speak powerful words of affirmation and love to our granddaughter and could tell it was something our daughter was yearning for in her heart. Thank goodness I have a wife who is sensitive to this, or I would probably fail to speak them at all. I guess I just assume that my actions of provision, protection, and faithful commitment automatically tell my children that I love them. Unfortunately, that isn't how things work. They need to hear my words in order to internalize the things I believe about them, words that tell them that I love them, am proud of them, and believe in them. Never underestimate the power of your spoken words. Your kids (and wife) need to hear the words "I love you" at least once every day. If they don't hear those words, they won't know.

Regardless of what your actions show them, if they don't hear you say that you love them, they will not really believe that you do. Kids need to hear this often—every day. Multiple times a day is better. Even if it feels stilted or uncomfortable, practice saying things that uplift your children numerous times daily. A good rule of thumb is to try to provide at least five "put-ups" for every negative thing you say. I've heard statistics that it needs to be maybe double that number to be truly effective. But if you come from an environment where positive things were never said, you're better off starting at an attainable goal. Otherwise you might get discouraged and give up. Trust me, the effort counts. Your kids don't expect perfection. They just want to know you care.

We have a toddler running our home right now. Due to her frenetically curious nature, I can't tell you how many times each day I find myself telling her, "No!" or "Don't!" or "Stop that!" That means I am trying to say a lot of positive affirmations to offset all those negatives.

The words spoken to children by people important to them are often taken as fact, even if they are not true. So we have to be careful of the words we use and how we use them. Your son probably wouldn't believe he was a garbage can no matter how many times someone else told him he was one. But he would believe he was *garbage* if you told him he was enough times. He probably wouldn't believe other people if they told him he was stupid, either. But he would definitely believe he was stupid if *you* told him he was, no matter how intelligent he actually is.

Fathers have an incredible influence (positive or negative) on nearly every aspect of their daughter's lives as well. Because a daughter so yearns to secure the love of her father, she believes what her father believes about her. If he calls her stupid or incompetent, she will believe that about herself. But if he calls her intelligent, beautiful, competent, and accomplished, she will believe that to be true as well. Her father determines how a girl feels about herself. If a father shows his daughter love, respect, and appreciation for who she is, she will believe that about herself as a woman, no matter what anyone else thinks. That's a powerful responsibility, guys. I can't tell you how many people I meet who are walking around with hurtful words imbedded in their hearts that their father spoke to them. As men we often don't think about what we say before we say it. Words don't mean as much to us as a person's actions do. But our words mean a lot to our children.

Merely the tone of our voice makes a big difference in how the message is received as well. Words said loudly, sarcastically, or in anger are interpreted one way by children. You can speak the same words gently or in love and they mean something entirely different. Our true inner feelings and attitude always come out in the words we speak.

Finally, I'm convinced the greatest communication tool we have as parents is to apologize and ask for forgiveness when we are wrong. This can be difficult for many people—myself included. But apologizing does not erode our authority—it develops respect for us from our children. Our children know when we are wrong. When we refuse to acknowledge that and repent, whether we err or sin, it makes us look overbearing, stubborn, and maybe downright ignorant.

Healthy Physical Affection

People from abusive backgrounds are often uncomfortable with too much (or any) physical affection. Healthy (nonsexual) physical affection is extremely important in developing healthy children. Your kids need to be hugged and kissed by their parents frequently. I was raised in a home without very much physical affection. As I got older, I realized how much I missed that in my life. When my children were born, I made a vow that I would give them plenty of physical affection even if it was difficult to do so. And it was! I often had to force myself to hug and kiss them, because it wasn't modeled for me as a child. I wasn't used to it—it was uncomfortable. I had to develop those neural pathways in my brain that made those actions more comfortable. As my children got older, it became easier, and with my granddaughter, it now feels like second nature.

Hug and kiss your kids. Give them plenty of physical love. Even as they get older, continue to show them physical affection. When my son was about thirteen years old, he hit a growth spurt and ended up taller than me—he became a great big old horse. Once when we were walking through the parking lot to go into a store he reached over and held my hand. My instantaneous reaction was to want to jerk my hand away. Because, you know, men don't hold hands in public, right? And he was bigger than me. But thankfully, I checked that reaction. Because he was not a man, he was a boy—my boy. So we held hands throughout the store, casually taking our time. We got some funny looks, but who cares. For whatever reason, he needed to hold his dad's hand. I was privileged to be able to fulfill that desire.

Our daughters need physical affection just as much as our sons, especially from Dad. Girls crave healthy masculine physical affection. If they don't get it at home from Dad, they will eventually seek it out from someone else—probably someone you don't want giving her physical affection. That said, at some point (maybe puberty), her desire to have Dad touch her might wane. As hormones and the confusion of her impending sexuality flood her body, she may not want anyone touching her. This happened with our daughter. Our little girl, who previously used to wrestle on the living room rug with me, entered adolescence and became moody, sullen, and standoffish. At about fourteen when the aliens invaded her body, she didn't want anyone touching her (especially me or her brother). But by eighteen, when the aliens suddenly vanished, she was back to her old affectionate self again.

Don't allow your past to keep you from giving the powerful gift of physical affection to your children. If you didn't have it growing up, you know how much you missed it. Like everything in this book, it takes courage to overcome this barrier. But your children deserve a loving parent and the opportunity to start life out on a healthy platform.

Praying for Your Children

The best action you can take for your children is to pray for them on a consistent basis. There are often situations where, as parents, all we can do is pray for our children. If you've ever had a child in the hospital to undergo an operation, you know the feeling of helplessness that accompanies that circumstance. Or having a teenage daughter out on a date past curfew. Or an adult son who gets involved in drugs and refuses to come home. Or a child who is lost in the woods. These are all situations where, as a parent, about all we can do is pray for divine intervention. Praying for them consistently not only asks for God's intervention in their lives but it also teaches them and us about spirituality.

Our model of faith is always more powerful than our words of faith. If you live a life of godly service in humility and faith, your children will internalize those values. If you live a hypocritical spiritual life, where you look good on the outside but criticize and complain about others and never do anything to serve others outside the doors of the church, you will pass that attitude on to your kids as well (or they will see it and reject your faith). If you have never risked anything for your faith, your children have probably never seen God answer your prayers.

So how do we share our faith and prayer life with our children? Look for everyday examples or situations from your past where you can openly and honestly share your faith and how God has worked in your life. Don't be afraid to let your kids know you made mistakes. Our kids know we are not perfect, and so telling them where you have struggled in life and why God's presence was helpful is very important. One of the blessings of being in full-time ministry is that God is faithful to show me and our children the fruits of my labor on a nearly daily basis. It is hard to argue with the concrete facts and reality of God's actions. Parents have a propensity to turn things into lectures. But sometimes less is more and actions always speak louder than words. Our example of living a godly life is a much more powerful message than any lecture could ever be.

Prayer is a powerful tool that parents have at their disposal. Let your children see and hear you pray. Pray with them at meals and at bedtime. Pray consistently for your child's spiritual, emotional, physical, and psychological health and safety. Pray God would bring healthy mentors and good friends into their lives. Pray for their sexual purity. Pray for their future spouses (and their parents). Pray for wisdom and discernment. And pray for your child's decision making. When our kids were teenagers, my wife prayed daily that our children would get "caught." She knew that they *would* make mistakes and poor choices, but if they got caught the first time they did something wrong, it would prevent them from harm or continuing until the consequences were serious. I believe God answered those prayers, as our teens were continually baffled that they always got caught whenever they strayed from the path.

Many men and women find being a spiritual leader in the home difficult. But prayer is one way you can powerfully lead your family spiritually. A father's or mother's prayers for their children are powerful. I heard a story on the radio some time ago. Every night a young girl's father came in and tucked her in bed, knelt down next to her bed, placed his hand on her head, and prayed aloud for God's blessing over her. This happened every night until she grew up and went away to college. One Christmas the girl was home visiting. As she sat at the kitchen table talking to her mother, she casually said, "Daddy still prays for me every night, doesn't he?" Her mother, shocked, said, "Well, yes he does. How did you know?" The girl replied, "I can still see his knee marks in the carpet next to my bed."

What kind of choices do you think that girl made while away in college, knowing that her father was interceding daily on her behalf with the Creator of the universe? My guess is, she probably thought a lot about the choices she made. Let me ask you this: how many of you were raised with a parent who prayed for you every day? If you are like most of the people I speak to, a small percentage of you were blessed to have a parent who did this. Let me ask you another question: how do you think your life might have been different if you *had* had a parent who prayed for you every day? I think my life would have been vastly different. If you pray for them daily, your kids' lives will be different too.

9

Thoughts for Women

Why You Matter

The hand that rocks the cradle is the hand that rules the world.

—W. R. Wallace

Ladies, as moms you are so special and so important in so many ways to so many people. Your family desperately needs you to be healed and whole. Since many of you reading this struggle with why your life is of value, here are just some brief thoughts on the importance you play in the lives of people around you.

To Your Son

Moms teach boys things they need to learn in order to be successful in life. Her model teaches him emotions such as empathy, compassion, tenderness, sensitivity, and love. He learns about sacrifice, gentleness, caring, and unconditional love from observing her live her life. His mother is the example of a woman, a wife, and a mother that he carries with him for his entire life. She is the major role model for femininity, how a woman loves a man, how a woman allows herself to be treated by a man, and healthy female sexuality. Mothers are often the barometer of a man's perception of how much respect a woman deserves from a man. Boys are consciously aware of the way their mothers treat their fathers. This often determines (consciously or unconsciously) the way they expect to be treated by their wives—and often influences the way they themselves treat their own wives.

Not only that, but a boy's mother has a huge influence on how a boy sees himself as a man. She can short-circuit the fragile connection between boyhood and manhood with her words and attitude. A mother who despises men can make life difficult for a boy. Especially for women who have been hurt by men in their life, this can present a real challenge for a boy.

On the other hand, a mother who respects and admires healthy masculinity can make a boy believe he was created for greatness. Through her affirming power, she can lift him up to be and do things he could never become or accomplish without her powerful influence in his life. Either way, a man's mother has a huge influence in his life and on his masculinity.

To Your Daughter

Mothers are the first and most important female role model in a young woman's life. You teach her things such as what authentic femininity looks like, how a woman loves a man, how much respect she gives a man, and how a woman should expect to be treated by a man. You show her what a marriage relationship with a man looks like and what authentic female sexuality looks like and how it behaves. For girls without that model, loving and living with a man can be a confusing proposition. You are also your daughter's model on what a mother is—how she acts, what she does, how she loves and nurtures her children. This is fundamental for the development of young girls into healthy women. A mother teaches a girl what a woman's roles are in life, how to fulfill those roles, and what healthy femininity looks like. A mother also models to her daughter what a woman's role is in marriage. A happy, secure, and confident wife teaches her daughters good things about men and relationships.

What does her mother's influence and example mean to a woman's choices in life? Did her mother allow herself to be used or abused by men? Did she have a healthy self-image? What did she feel about the masculine gender? Did she like them or did she have bitterness and loathing for men in general? A woman's mother is the directional beacon that guides a female through the early stages of life and is the first model she has of how a woman deals with marriage, men, family, and life. Because a girl bases the value of a woman on what is modeled by her mother and on the respect her father extends to his wife, she needs to respect her mother.

A mother's influence may also have a great deal to do with the type of men her daughter attracts and is attracted to. She certainly modeled how a woman should expect to be treated by a man, how a woman responds to a man, how a woman mothers her children, how a woman carries herself, how a woman acts and dresses, and how a woman deals with life. If a girl admires and looks up to her mom, and thinks she got a good deal in the man she chose, then she's been blessed. If not, she may need to recognize how her mom influenced her perspective on these issues and seek to change how she responds in her relationships and toward life's challenges.

To Your Husband

You are special to your husband because you empower him to be more than he could ever be on his own. My young adult son once asked me how he would know when the "right" woman came along. After thinking about it, my best advice to him was that this woman would make him want to be a better man. He would feel compelled to accomplish something with his life in order to make her proud of him. She would encourage him to strive for success merely by her presence. He would *want* to work hard and improve himself in order to provide a better life for her, for her approval.

Women have an incredible influence in men's lives. The old saying "Behind every good man is a good woman" is not just hyperbole, it is the truth. A woman can use her powerful influence to subtly guide and lift a man up to be all he was created for. She holds the key to his success or failure as a man, husband, and father. This influence is delicate, understated, and nurturing as opposed to a male's bolder, more overt influence. It tantalizes a man with heady inspiration and inspires him to believe in himself, to believe he possesses greatness.

Her subtle, refined grace arouses within him a passion that emboldens his character and deeds.

A woman can be a huge influence in a man's life, especially as an encourager. There are few things that an authentically masculine man will not attempt to accomplish or persevere through if he knows he has a supportive wife or woman who believes in him. He will withstand anything life dishes out if he has his wife there to encourage him. There are few defeats or failures he cannot endure with the positive support of his treasured wife. A man whose wife respects him walks proud and confident into the world. In fact, a man often equates respect with love. The more his wife respects him, the more he feels loved by her. A man always feels like he is being judged by life. If his wife rates him highly, it doesn't matter much what the rest of the world thinks.

You are also special because of your ability to be a life-giver and caretaker. Genesis 2:18 says, "It is not good for the man to be alone. I will make a helper suitable for him." Clearly, men fare better in life when they have a helpmate, a companion, and a completer by their side.

As we discussed in chapter 8, single men have earlier and higher mortality rates than married men. Men who find themselves single either through bachelorhood, death of a spouse, or divorce do not fare as well as men who are married, by any measurable category. Married men are healthier and live longer than single men do—they are at much less risk of having a stroke. Married men have a 46 percent lower rate of dying from cardiovascular disease than unmarried men. The death rate and risks of medical problems such as hypertension, heart attacks, and strokes increase for men who are divorced. Married men also have much better mental health than their single counterparts, and single men engage in an unhealthier lifestyle, evidenced in at least one instance by the fact that they consume about twice as much alcohol as married men. Most men in prison are single and most crimes are committed by men who are unmarried.

Men are not meant to be alone. They need women to complete and grow their lives. You have been uniquely created by God to have amazing nurturing and relationship skills.

And you are special to your husband because you make him a better father. You can make him a hero in the eyes of his children, and you can garner him more respect from them than he could ever get on his own. And when he has your genuine respect and admiration, there's almost nothing he won't try to accomplish.

To Your Family

God designed you as a woman to be more nurturing than a man. Without your gifts in this area, a family would never be able to survive, much less thrive. Women are a lot more tenderhearted than men. Women are more gentle and caring about people and their feelings. Women tend to be more unconditional in their love, while men are more performance-based in theirs. Women are generally more accepting of others and their faults than men are. Women are more apt to fall for a sob story or try to rescue someone who claims to have been mistreated. They are more attuned to their emotions and sensitive to nuances and shifts in relationships.

A woman has the capability of being empathetic whenever anyone is feeling bad, comforting when they are wounded, and healing when they are in pain. She is more often than not caring, kind, thoughtful, gentle, tender, compassionate, loving, and sensitive. She feels compelled to make sure the children are safe, fed properly, washed, and clean, with all their needs met. Her presence helps children thrive and grow like vigorous stalks of corn in fertile soil. Her nurturing instincts bring vitality to family life. Her healing touch cures everything from scraped knees to bruised egos. Her gentle compassion soothes even the most horrendous betrayal.

Women love to encourage and support other people in their search for meaning in their lives. They love to share their life experiences with one another. They like to help others with their problems.

Women are the nurturers of the family that keep it functioning and growing. Frankly, the mortality rate would probably be a lot higher if men were left alone to their own devices with their children.

There's a great line in the movie *The Boys Are Back*, starring Clive Owen. A widower and his two sons are grieving over the death of their wife and mother. As they struggle to survive, one of them sadly makes the statement, "We're just like *Home Alone*, only there's three of us."

Mom—you are very special if for no other reason than you are a giver of life. It is a powerful role that God created you for. Never forget that.

Spiritually

Mothers tend to be the ones who first expose their children to church and God. In fact, females in general seem to be what attract men to church. How many young men have started coming to church and accepted Christ because a young gal they were interested in went to church? How many men have eventually come to Christ because of the example their wives set in their lives? I know many.

Women, I think, tend to have a larger, deeper, and perhaps more personal relationship with God than do most men. They are more willing to submit to his omniscience and humble themselves before him. They probably hold him in greater awe than men do (or at least are willing to admit through their actions). It has been my observation that women tend to pray and worship more deeply than men do. Look around in church during a worship service—it is most often the women with their hands raised, their eyes closed, and tears streaming down their faces. They are able to let themselves go easier into communion with the Holy Spirit. Perhaps because they are more relational and intuitive, they may be able to access the Holy Spirit more easily than men.

It seems that life's challenges tend to bring women closer to God but push men further away. When life beats me down, my initial response is to come out swinging at everyone and everything, including God. My wife's response is to get on her knees and pray.

Because women are more relational, I think they tend to have a deeper relationship with God. They are probably more able to love or be *in* love with the masculine image of a heavenly Father than most men are. While I fear God greatly (which is the beginning of wisdom) and I feel like I have a close relationship with him, I generally do not feel like he is my "lover," my husband, the lover of my soul, my soulmate, or any of the other terms of endearment that worship songs attribute to him. That probably closes off a certain intimacy in our relationship that a woman might be able to access more readily. Perhaps having the gift of creating and carrying life develops a deeper connection with the Creator himself.

Moms, you matter.

10

Thoughts for Men

Why You Matter

Sherman made the terrible discovery that men make about
their fathers sooner or later . . . that the man before him was
not an aging father but a boy, a boy much like himself, a
boy who grew up and had a child of his own and, as best
he could, out of a sense of duty and, perhaps love, adopted
a role called Being a Father so that his child would have
something mythical and infinitely important: a Protector,
who would keep a lid on all the chaotic and catastrophic
possibilities of life.

—Tom Wolfe

Dads, you are equally as important as moms, just in different
ways. First of all, you are the leaders of your families. You
might be reluctant to assume that role. You might even deny
that it falls to you. Nonetheless, you *are* your family's de facto

leader, whether you choose to believe it or not. Regardless of what the media, the educational system, your children's peers, or famous celebrities try to inject into your child's mind and heart, your influence as his father supersedes all those other influences.

Here's why. You may not think of yourself as being particularly influential or even successful at life. Maybe you don't make a lot of money, lead a large group of people, save lives, or invent amazing gadgets. Maybe life has even beaten you down and you've lost confidence in your abilities. Consequently, you don't think of yourself as a big deal. But you can bet your kids do. They think you're a very big deal. They don't know or care what the outside world thinks. They only know that, within the four walls of your home, you are about the biggest, wisest, most powerful person alive. Oh, they know that you're not perfect. But they don't care, because you're just good enough to be indispensable in their lives.

Here are some ways that you matter in the loves of your loved ones:

To Your Son

Sons learn a number of skills from their fathers that allow them to successfully navigate life. They need men (hopefully their father) to model certain life skills for them in order to assimilate them into their lives. Without that role model many boys are left to figure out life on their own—a very difficult process. The following are just some of the areas that a young man needs modeled for him by an older man or men.

How to live life: One of the great things about men is they know stuff. They know how to do things and how the world works. They learn from their experiences and from trial and error. They learn from being taught by the important men in their lives. Being *capable* is important to our self-esteem as men and boys. If no one shows us how to do something, how can we ever learn to be capable? And if we do not feel capable, how can we feel good about our manhood? Sons learn from fathers how the world works, how to successfully live in it, and the skills necessary to succeed in life.

How to solve problems: Boys and young men also need to be tested as part of the maturation process. Fathers are in a unique position to apply the pressure necessary to their sons to develop character. Young men who never test themselves against life never find out what they are made of. They never become confident and secure in their manhood. Trials mature a man in ways that books or lectures never can. If boys are rescued (typically by female mentors) too often growing up, they never learn self-reliance and the skills to succeed in life. Most often a boy needs a man to help teach him to navigate his way through the brambles and thornbushes of manhood. Without that guidance, too many young boys and men grow up angry, frustrated, anxious, and scared. Too often they compensate for that by exhibiting a false sense of bravado and self-confidence. I remember as a young man being angry, defensive, and brash as a way to cover my insecurities. I was insecure because I never had a father figure guide me and teach me how to solve life's problems.

The truth is, if we continue to produce greater and greater numbers of angry young men, we will eventually experience an apocalyptic meltdown within our culture. When boys do not learn how to solve problems in life, they rely on others to take care of them instead of fulfilling their roles as protector and provider to the people they are responsible for. This failure then contributes even more to them feeling like a disappointment in life.

How a man faces the world: Boys need men to teach them how the world works. As a former (and hopefully future) middle school and high school basketball coach, I think one of the things my players appreciated the most was me letting them know the expectations I had for them. I provided leadership by telling them clearly and in no uncertain terms when they were doing something right and more importantly when they were doing something wrong. That's how all of us (especially males) learn. When we do not understand what is expected of us, we are mired in uncertainty and ambiguity. Boys especially thrive when they know their boundaries. It's one of the reasons sports are so attractive to them. The rules are the same for everyone, there are no exceptions, and the consequences of failing to abide by those rules are clear. It levels the playing field and allows young men to thrive. As a coach I always wanted to teach a bigger lesson than just the skills and fundamentals of the game. I wanted to teach life lessons every chance I got. I am blessed that many former players approach me and tell me the difference I have made in their lives.

Fathers and discipline: Fathers are especially important in disciplining children. Fathers seem to have been endowed by God with the mantle of authority within the family. Children have an innate fear of fathers that they do not have toward their mothers. Especially for teen boys, fathers are the boundary that keeps them from asserting their will in ways that could be destructive to themselves and others. Fathers are routinely viewed as the enforcer of family rules and values. You seldom see gang members with involved, loving fathers at home. Teenage boys may even start to get mouthy with Mom at this stage in ways they would never try with their father.

Boys who are not disciplined by their fathers do not learn self-discipline, which is a huge factor in male satisfaction in life. Boys who are undisciplined are unhappy and grow up to be men who disappoint others, especially those close to them.

How to love a woman: Fathers are instrumental in modeling how a man is supposed to love a woman. This is not something that comes naturally to most males. Merely watch the difference in how a young man who grew up with no healthy male role models treats his wife (or more often live-in lover) versus one who grew up with a father who loved his mother. To give oneself sacrificially for the sake of another is not a natural male trait. In fact, the opposite might generally be true.

Loving a woman is a modeled behavior for a male. Learning to lead his family in a healthy manner is another modeled behavior that boys seldom learn from any other source. The respect that a father gives a boy's mother is the level of respect that he will think all women deserve. Appreciating the value that a woman brings to a relationship and the family is another gift that a father gives to his son. Learning to cherish and love a woman in the ways that she needs and not the ways that he feels more comfortable with is a lesson that boys cannot get from any other venue than from watching their father every day. Recognizing her more tender heart and the devastation that his words can have on a woman are taught to a boy by his father. And perhaps the greatest lesson he passes along is the ability to admit he is wrong, apologize, and ask for forgiveness.

Without the modeled behavior from a father, boys are left to try to navigate through life and all of the difficult circumstances that they will be faced with. Boys without fathers are at a big disadvantage in every area of life. Many never recover and so spread destruction and pain wherever they go. Those who do recover struggle with issues their entire lives. Fatherhood wounds are deep, jagged tears in a boy's chest that leave scar tissue in their wake.

To Your Daughter

Fathers have been given a tremendous ability to influence the lives of their daughters. A father provides a huge role model for his daughter regarding the qualities she looks for in men and the standards she maintains. He is the first man in her life and models how a man should treat a woman, how a man should act, and how a man shows healthy love and affection to a woman. He also sets the standard for how a daughter feels she deserves to be treated by men. He even determines how a girl feels about herself.

Fathers have a huge impact on the intellectual, emotional, and physical development of their daughters as well. Toddlers with father attachments have better problem-solving skills.[1] Girls with close father relationships achieve higher academic success.[2] As they get older, father-connectedness is the number one factor in delaying and preventing girls from engaging in premarital sex and abusing drugs and alcohol. Girls with involved fathers are more assertive and have higher self-esteem.[3] And girls with involved fathers also have higher quantitative and verbal skills and higher intellectual functioning.[4]

Fathers who are active, loving, positive role models in their daughters' lives provide them with the opportunity to use those character traits as a measuring tape for future men in their lives. The way in which a man treats his wife speaks volumes to a girl on how she should expect to be treated and valued by men later in her life. If her father shows that he values her mother as someone worthy of love and respect, a girl will expect that for herself from her husband. If he exhibits a model of abuse or disrespect for her mother, a girl may feel that she deserves to be treated that way as a wife as well.

And if her father shows his daughter love, respect, and appreciation for who she is, she will believe that about herself as a woman, no matter what anyone else thinks.

A little girl who has her father's love knows what it's like to be unconditionally and completely adored by a man. She knows the feeling of safety that love creates.[5]

Conversely, men who abandon or abuse their daughters set them up for a lifetime of pain, distrust, and feelings of worthlessness. When men are angry or disrespectful to the females in their families, it sets their daughters up to expect this kind of treatment from all men. If a man does not provide for and protect them, they have no expectations of this behavior from the men they enter into relationships with. Why would a woman willingly marry a man who can't or won't hold a job to support his family? Why would she marry a man who abuses or abandons her? She probably wouldn't do it intentionally. Perhaps that was the type of man that was modeled for her growing up and she is subconsciously attracted to that model, believing she deserves that kind of treatment and is unworthy of anything better.

Another area that a woman's father plays a major role in is her sexual decision-making process. For instance, girls with uninvolved or absent fathers tend to become sexually active at an earlier age than their fathered peers. They also have a greater number of sexual partners. Women who have not had a model of healthy masculinity in their lives often have trouble detecting predators, abusers, and men who will abandon them. They are in some ways like a lamb left to the wolves. Oftentimes, these women continue to choose the same type of men, getting the same results over and over again.

Think you don't matter, Dad? Think again.

To Your Wife

As a husband you meet many needs of your wife. Perhaps most importantly, a wife has a need to know she is loved and wanted. She needs to be reassured of that often. If you are not giving her words that confirm your love or showing her through your deeds often enough that you love her, she will become *needy*. This isn't the moping around, desperate-for-compliments kind of needy, but more like a plant that hasn't been watered for a while needy. The thing all women want to know is, "Does he still love me?" With men, what we *do* always speaks louder than what we *say*. All men know you judge a man by his actions, not his words. Men only spend time doing things they care about, regardless of what they may say. If we love something (fishing, hunting, fixing up old cars, etc.), we spend time on it. If we don't like something (going to church, shopping, cooking, cleaning house, etc.), we don't spend any more time than necessary doing it. So if we *say* we love our wife but don't spend any time with her, we are sending a mixed message.

All women desperately yearn to know they are beautiful. Beauty is at the heart of all womanhood. God made the female face and body to be adored and even lusted after by the male of the species. All women want to know they are beautiful. Even more than want, they *need* to know they are desired and beautiful. Women often develop their self-esteem through their relationships and their physical appearance. God created each woman naturally beautiful. Guys, tell your wife frequently (every day) that she is beautiful and that you love her. She needs to hear it (even if you've said it a thousand times), and you'll be glad you did.

Finally, a husband's role is also to provide cover—to take the brunt of life. One of the effects we see of being a single mom is that they get beaten down by life. They have to face life and all its problems by themselves. They have no one to help them or share the responsibilities, make decisions, enforce rules, or do chores. I even hear ultrafeminist women complain about having to bear all of life's burdens—having to make *all* the decisions. Guys, shelter your wife from the hardships of life. It's not that she isn't an equal partner, it's just that you have been better designed and equipped to be able to shoulder those burdens for your family.

To Your Family

Being a father is hard. It may be the most difficult thing I've ever done. And it doesn't seem to get any easier. The older my kids get, the more difficult and complicated the issues seem to be. My experiences with one child seldom seem relevant to the next child. And what works well in one situation rarely applies to the next.

But all things that are truly meaningful and significant are hard. And the more significant they are, the more difficult they become. So it goes without saying that if fathering is the most difficult thing you've ever done, it's probably because it's the most important and significant role you'll ever have. Certainly, as a father you are indispensable and irreplaceable in the lives of your children in ways that are unimaginable. Here are several ways you are important to your family:

As a provider: Providing for our children is one of the earliest and most basic roles that men have fulfilled. For most of human history, the man's role was to hunt and provide sustenance for his family. After hunter-gatherers phased out, men farmed, and after the industrial revolution they went to work in factories, but always under the umbrella of providing. This role is ingrained in us as men to the point that if we do not provide it, it often affects us in profound ways. But sometimes providing consists of more than just working longer or harder.

As a protector: A big part of my role as a father is protecting my children. Not only physically, but also mentally and emotionally. Dads need to be tough in order to guard their homes and keep their families safe. Our kids look up to us to provide for and protect them. I was at the doctor's office today.

A little girl (under two?) was there getting a shot. As she received the injection, she started crying, "Daddy, Daddy!" Afterward she wanted Mommy to console and nurture her, but her initial instinct was to cry for Daddy to protect her from harm and pain.

Dads not only need to be physically tough but emotionally tough too. That's because Dad provides not only physical protection but also guards against unhealthy mental and emotional attacks. But being physically tough and domestically tough are two different things. Many dads are physically tough guys who would not hesitate to fight for their kids but back off and don't protect their children from the culture rushing in to grab them. When Dad is passive, apathetic, embarrassed to intervene, or even just nonchalant about the cultural influences entering his home, he is allowing himself to be "tied up" so that his home can be plundered.

For instance, many parents are uncomfortable interfering with the friends their children choose. But friends can do great damage. Many a parent has seen twenty years of hard work flushed down the toilet by their child spending twenty minutes around the wrong person. You wouldn't consider allowing a child to have access to a medicine cabinet full of poisonous drugs. So why would you allow them unlimited access to friends who could be just as dangerous to their health as any chemical? You also wouldn't allow your older children to hang around with pimps or drug pushers, but some of the young people they go to school with are apprenticing for those jobs even now.

Too much exposure to media is also detrimental to kids. Social media, television, and computer video games, used in excess, are damaging to developing young brains. Not to mention the addictive capabilities of pornography.

Dad, you need to be active in monitoring the outside influences that are reaching out to your children. They need you—even if they protest that they don't.

As a provisionary: A provisioner does not just provide materially for those under his safeguard. While providing for the material needs (food, shelter, clothing, etc.) of his charges is part of his role, this responsibility goes even deeper. It also involves anticipating possible or expected future needs and then providing for those needs, whether they are material, emotional, psychological, or physical. It means having a "provision"—the ability to see beyond today's circumstances and into the future. Such needs might include the more obvious, such as college funds for the kids, money for your daughter's wedding, or retirement savings. Or they might be more intangible, such as anticipating (even before she does) your wife's unspoken need to go back to college to finish a degree at some point and having the funds and your schedule arranged to allow it to happen. Or anticipating that your children may go through dangerous activities during adolescence, such as drugs, eating disorders, or self-harm, and educating yourself beforehand so that you are prepared to deal with them effectively *before* they happen. Or possibly anticipating that you may end up raising your grandchildren someday. Being a provisioner means, as a man, that you are not stupid—even if our society expects you to be.

I can't think of any phase of fathering that I have been through that has been particularly easy. Frankly, the older my kids get, the harder it becomes. It's difficult being a father and raising a family. It's difficult leading a family, especially today. But your family relies upon your strength. They cannot thrive without your presence and masculine essence. Your protection and provision keep them safe from harm, and your presence keeps them bonded and secure.

Spiritually

Fathers are one of the most important factors in how children develop their spirituality, not only in teaching their children, but in how they model their faith. But fathers are also the biggest key to whether or not children even develop faith. A large study conducted by the Swiss government revealed some startling facts regarding generational transmission of faith and religious values:

1. If both father and mother attend church regularly, 33 percent of their children will end up as regular churchgoers, and 41 percent will end up attending irregularly.

2. If the father is irregular and the mother regular, only 3 percent of the children will subsequently become regulars themselves, while a further 59 percent will become irregulars.

3. If the father is nonpracticing and the mother regular, only 2 percent of children will become regular worshipers, and 37 percent will attend irregularly.

4. If the father attends regularly and the mother irregularly or not at all, between 38 and 44 percent of children became regular attendees.[6]

This is not to suggest that Mom is not important in the spiritual development of children, but perhaps that children take cues about domestic life from their mothers and conceptions of the outside world from their fathers. It appears that if Dad takes God seriously, then his children do as well.[7]

Whether you want the job or not, whether you feel qualified or not—Dad, you *are* the theology professor in your home. You set the spiritual tone and foundation in your home and likely the belief system your children adopt—at least until they are old enough to develop their own, which they will have to eventually. Every day you are teaching your kids about God, faith, truth, and the Bible through your actions and words. Didn't think you were signing up for that when you decided to become a father, did you? And unfortunately for you, once you are in this position, you can't resign.[8] Because even your resignation will teach your kids something about faith. And being passive or apathetic about your spiritual walk teaches them even more.

One of the functions of faith and religion is to remind people that they are not God. It is through the process of acknowledging and worshiping an omnipotent being greater than you that develops humility, faith, and strength of character. That's healthy for a variety of reasons, not the least of which is that it keeps us from believing we are our own god. Not only that, but recognizing and worshiping a holy God helps keep kids from becoming self-focused. Little children already intuitively seem to know about God. They are in awe of all they see and recognize a certain spiritual element in the world that adults seem to miss. Being in submission to a superior being is a healthy way to live.

Dads are uniquely qualified to teach their kids that lesson. Men, remember one thing—you matter. Our world likes to tear men and fathers down, portraying us as bumbling idiots. But no man on the face of the earth is more important to your children than you are. And no man has more influence over your family than you do. Don't waste that influence.

Conclusion

Better Parents, Better Families, Better World

"The deepest principle in human nature is the craving to be appreciated." From infancy right through old age, in our own ways we're all asking the same questions: "Does anyone love me?" "Am I special to someone?" "Am I appreciated?" It's a shame that so many children grow up without getting affirmative answers to those questions.

—William James, Harvard professor

At our ministry, Better Dads, we have a saying, "Better Parents = Better Families = Better World." We believe that by educating, mentoring, and empowering parents to be better moms and dads, we can help develop better families. And better families definitely translate into a better world.

As parents you have the greatest influence on your children of anybody on the planet. So many parents are concerned about outside influences, but study after study shows that the people with the most influence in a child's life (even teenagers) are their parents. In case no one has ever told you, *You Are Important.* Some may laugh at that, but some of you didn't know. Maybe you have teens and you think they are more influenced by video and movie stars than by their parents. Those entities certainly can have negative influence as your children reach adolescence, but your healthy and life-giving influence can counterbalance and eventually offset that. Studies also show that kids and teens who spend time with their parents have better self-esteem and better interpersonal communication skills.

It's a stereotype that teenagers do not want to spend time with their parents. MTV performed an in-depth seven-month study of thirteen- to twenty-four-year-olds in 2007 and asked them, "What one thing in life makes you most happy?" The biggest answer by far was "Spending time with friends, family, and loved ones."[1] That means you have more influence than anyone else in their lives.

But that means that we have to be willing and courageous enough to actually use that influence. If we are absent too often or are afraid to exert our values and ideals on our children, we lose that influence and waste the opportunity to teach them valuable life lessons. And if we allow our past wounds to dictate the way we parent, we also waste that precious gift of influencing the lives of our children in positive ways.

Please also recognize that your words have great power with your children. They'll remember many of your comments for years to come. In fact, their whole outlook on life could be shaped—for better or for worse—by something you say. Even in everyday life, your children will respond much better to positive words than they will to criticism, preaching at them, or nagging them to do what you want. Instead, whenever possible, use words intentionally to bless and to build up, whether you yell those positive words, whisper them, or simply speak them as a normal part of the day.

And lest we forget, a mother and father working together are more powerful than any individual parent. When a man and a woman use their own strengths to compensate for their partner's weaknesses, they become much more powerful as a team than they are as individuals. I encourage you as a team to develop a plan to intentionally teach your values to your children. Oftentimes when we react (instead of being proactive) to life, we miss or mishandle teaching moments. Your sons and daughters need all your help and experiences to successfully become the men and women that God created them to be.

Final Words

Finally, don't quit! Never give up! You are more precious and valuable than you will ever know. Your children need you no matter how old they are or how many mistakes you've made. And regardless of what anyone has ever told you, YOU MATTER! People love you and depend upon you more than you will ever realize. You have a lot to offer the world. The challenges you have endured and overcome have made you uniquely qualified to help others who are going through the same heartaches. God does have a plan for your life. Your past is the past. It's time to become all that you were meant to be.

Break those generational cycles. That's the way to win and get justice for what was perpetrated upon you. You triumph by being the kind of parents for your children that you deserved as a child. The best revenge is living life well. I am proud of you—be blessed and have a good life!

Acknowledgments

As with any book, the majority of the credit goes to those working behind the scenes. People in positions as editors, copywriters, advertising and marketing people, publicity, sales staff, administration, art and graphic design, warehouse personnel, and acquisitions all labor tirelessly and seldom get the credit they deserve. I hesitate to mention names because I do not want to inadvertently leave anyone out, so I'll just thank everyone who works at Revell Books. I may not know you personally, but I do appreciate you immensely.

I'd also like to thank my personal Savior, Jesus Christ, for giving me healing and forgiveness. Without that grace and mercy, I hesitate to think where I might be today—quite likely dead or alone and addicted to any number of substances and vices. Certainly, I know I would not be blessed to have the family I have today and the privilege of using my life experiences to help others who find themselves in pain, fear, anger, and grief. Should you ever hear me complain about my lot in life, please feel free to remind me of God's blessed compassion upon me.

Finally, no book of mine gets published without a nod and wink to the love of my life, Suzanne. Without her, none of this is possible, nor would I care.

Notes

Chapter 1 When Parents Fail

1. Lucille Zimmerman, *Renewed* (Nashville: Abingdon Press, 2013), 156.

2. David Brooks, *The Social Animal: Hidden Sources of Love, Character, and Achievement* (New York: Random House, 2011).

3. Susan Forward, with Craig Buck, *Toxic Parents: Overcoming Their Hurtful Legacy and Reclaiming Your Life* (New York: Bantam Books, 1989 [paperback 2002]), 5.

4. Ibid., 169–70.

5. Lisa A. Miles, "Early Wounding & Dysfunctional Family Roles," World of Psychology, PsycheCentral, August 8, 2013, http://psych central.com/blog/archives/2013/08/10/early-wounding-dysfunctional -family-roles/.

6. Forward, with Buck, *Toxic Parents*, 15.

7. Claudia Black, "Understanding the Pain of Abandonment," *Psychology Today*, June 4, 2010, https://www.psychologytoday.com/blog/the -many-faces-addiction/201006/understanding-the-pain-abandonment.

8. Forward, with Buck, *Toxic Parents*, 93.

9. Ibid., 110.

10. Ronald Potter-Efron, *Healing the Angry Brain* (Oakland, CA: New Harbinger Publications, Inc., 2012), 71.

11. Forward, with Buck, *Toxic Parents*, 118.

12. Sandra D. Wilson, *Hurt People Hurt People* (Grand Rapids: Discovery House Publishers, 2001), 33.

13. Forward, with Buck, *Toxic Parents*, 113.

14. Ibid., 114.

15. Ibid., 139.

16. Ibid., 151, 154.

17. Ibid., 138.

18. "Munchausen Syndrome by Proxy," US National Library of Medicine, MedlinePlus, August, 22, 2013, http://www.nlm.nih.gov/medline plus/ency/article/001555.htm.

19. Ibid.

20. Tara Bahrampour, "Romanian Orphans Subjected to Deprivation Must Now Deal with Dysfunction," *Washington Post*, January 30, 2014, http://www.washingtonpost.com/local/romanian-orphans-subjected -to-deprivation-must-now-deal-with-disfunction/2014/01/30/a9dbea 6c-5d13-11e3-be07-006c776266ed_story.html.

21. Forward, with Buck, *Toxic Parents*, 79.

22. Ibid., 71.

23. Ibid., 71–72.

24. Ibid., 72.

25. Martha Stout, *The Sociopath Next Door* (New York: Broadway Books/Random House, 2005), 9.

26. Athena Dean Holtz, "Dealing with PTSD—So What Exactly Is PTSD and Who Does It Affect?" March 4, 2015, http://athenadeanholtz .com/dealing-with-ptsd-so-what-exactly-is-ptsd-and-who-does-it-affect/.

27. Athena Dean Holtz, "Dealing with PTSD—Adrenaline and Triggers: Part One—How Your Body Responds," March 13, 2015, http://athena deanholtz.com/dealing-with-ptsd-adrenaline-and-triggers-part-one-how -your-body-responds/.

Chapter 2 How Our Past Affects Our Own Parenting

1. Forward, with Buck, *Toxic Parents*, 6.

2. Ibid., 17.

3. "Definition of Dissociation," Medicinenet.com, March 19, 2012, http://www.medicinenet.com/script/main/art.asp?articlekey=38857.

4. "Dissociation FAQ's," International Society for the Study of Trauma and Dissociation, http://www.isst-d.org/?contentID=76.

5. Foundations Training for Caregivers: Session 3—Child Development and the Impact of Abuse, Oregon Dept. of Human Services, 7.

6. Donna Jackson Nakazawa, "7 Ways Childhood Adversity Can Change Your Brain," *Psychology Today*, August 7, 2015, https://www.psychologytoday.com/blog/the-last-best-cure/201508/7-ways-childhood-adversity-changes-your-brain.

7. "Impact of Child Abuse," Blue Knot Foundation, http://www.blueknot.org.au/WHAT-WE-DO/Resources/General-Information/Impact-of-child-abuse.

8. "Effects of Poverty, Hunger, and Homelessness on Children and Youth," American Psychological Association, http://www.apa.org/pi/families/poverty.aspx.

9. Gleaned from Ruby K. Payne, Philip E. DeVol, and Terie Dreussi Smith, *Bridges Out of Poverty* (Highlands, TX: aha! Process, Inc., 2005).

10. Gleaned from Ruby K. Payne, *Crossing the Tracks for Love* (Highlands, TX: aha! Process Inc., 2005).

11. Rick I. Johnson, *Romancing Your Better Half* (Grand Rapids: Revell, 2015), 129–31.

12. Scott Mendelson, "The Lasting Damage of Child Abuse," HuffPost Healthy Living, December, 31, 2013, http://www.huffingtonpost.com/scott-mendelson-md/the-lasting-damage-of-chi_b_4515918.html.

13. Laura Schlessinger, *Bad Childhood—Good Life* (New York: HarperCollins, 2006), 2.

14. Ibid., 23.

Chapter 3 Healing Our Wounds

1. Johnson, *Romancing Your Better Half*, 123–24.

2. Brooks, *Social Animal*, 239.

3. Roberta M. Gilbert, *The Eight Concepts of the Bowen Theory* (Stephens City, VA: Leading Systems Press, 2004), 1–2.

4. Ibid., 8–9.

5. Ibid., 27–32.

6. David Schnarch, *Passionate Marriage: Keeping Love & Intimacy Alive in Committed Relationships* (New York: W. W. Norton & Co., 2009), 51.

7. Ibid., 4.

8. Kendra Cherry, "Erikson's Psychosocial Stages Summary Chart," updated April 24, 2016, http://psychology.about.com/od/psychosocialtheories/fl/Psychosocial-Stages-Summary-Chart.htm.

9. Beth Moore, *Get Out of That Pit* (Nashville: Thomas Nelson, 2007), 44–45.

Chapter 4 Action Steps to Healing

1. Moore, *Get Out of That Pit*, 103.
2. Forward, with Buck, *Toxic Parents*, 229.
3. Ibid., 227.

Chapter 5 Healing Our Emotions

1. Brooks, *Social Animal*, 66.
2. Forward, with Buck, *Toxic Parents*, 217.
3. Ibid., 215–16.
4. Lucille Zimmerman, *Renewed* (Nashville: Abingdon Press, 2013), 123.
5. Ibid., 124.
6. Lorie Johnson, "The Deadly Consequences of Unforgiveness," CBN News Health & Science, June 22, 2015, http://www.cbn.com/cbnnews /healthscience/2015/June/The-Deadly-Consequences-of-Unforgiveness /?cpid=:ID:-2354-:DT:-2015-06-22-16:03:23-:US:-AB1-:CN:-CP1-:P O:-NC1-:ME:-SU1-:SO:-FB1-:SP:-7C1-:PF:-TX1-.
7. Ibid.
8. Moore, *Get Out of That Pit*, 37.

Chapter 6 New Parenting Strategies

1. Dave Ziegler, "Understanding and Helping Children Who Have Been Traumatized," Foundations Training for Caregivers: Session 5— Behavior Modification, Oregon Dept. of Human Services, 1–3.
2. Potter-Efron, *Healing the Angry Brain*, gleaned from chap. 4.
3. Ibid., 80.
4. Ibid., 83.
5. Gleaned from Brooks, *Social Animal*, 180–81.
6. Gleaned from ibid., 181.
7. Gleaned from ibid.
8. Gleaned from ibid., 182.
9. Forward, with Buck, *Toxic Parents*, 31.
10. The Nurturing Parenting Programs, "Abusive Parenting and Child-rearing Practices," Juvenile Justice Bulletin, November 2000, https:// www.ncjrs.gov/html/ojjdp/2000_11_1/page3.html.
11. Gleaned from Tim Elmore, "How to Fix Parenting Styles Which May Damage Your Kids," HowtoLearn.com, May 26, 2011, http://www

.howtolearn.com/2011/05/how-to-fix-parenting-styles-which-may-damage-your-kids/.

12. "The 10 Things Kids Need Most," Child, Youth, and Family, http://www.cyf.govt.nz/info-for-parents/the-ten-things-kids-need-most.html.

13. Brooks, *Social Animal*, 67.

Chapter 7 Good Kids, Bad Kids

1. Gleaned from Foundations Training for Caregivers: Session 5—Behavior Management, Oregon Dept. of Human Services.

2. Brett and Kay McKay, "Why You Should Parent Like a Video Game," Art of Manliness, August 19, 2014, http://www.artofmanliness.com/2014/08/19/why-you-should-parent-like-a-video-game/.

3. H. Stephen Glenn and Jane Nelsen, *Raising Self-Reliant Children in a Self-Indulgent World* (Roseville, CA: Prima Publishing, 2000), 145.

4. Gwen Dewar, "ADHD in Children: Are Millions Being Unnecessarily Medicated?" *Parenting Science*, last modified March 2013, http://www.parentingscience.com/ADHD-in-children.html.

5. Chris Bell, "Epigenetics: How to Alter Your Genes," *The Telegraph*, October 16, 2013, http://www.telegraph.co.uk/news/science/10369861/Epigenetics-How-to-alter-your-genes.html.

6. Laura Blue, "Childhood Trauma leaves Legacy of Brain Changes," *Time*, January 16, 2013, http://healthland.time.com/2013/01/16/childhood-trauma-leaves-legacy-of-brain-changes/.

Chapter 8 Healthy Relationship Practices

1. Linda J. Waite and Maggie Gallagher, *The Case for Marriage: Why Married People Are Happier, Healthier, and Better Off Financially* (New York: Broadway Book, 2000), 47–67.

2. Kay Hymowitz, W. Bradford Wilcox, and Kelleen Kaye, "The New Unmarried Moms," *Wall Street Journal*, March 15, 2013, http://online.wsj.com/article/SB10001424127887323826704578356494206134184.html.

3. Statistics gleaned from Rick I. Johnson, "Is There a Difference in Educational Outcomes in Students from Single Parent Homes?" a thesis presented to the graduate program in partial fulfillment of the requirements for the degree of Master's in Education, Concordia University Portland, 2009.

4. Center for Behavioral Intervention, "Protecting Your Children: Advice from Child Molesters," Beaverton, OR, gleaned from brochure.

5. Ibid.

6. Ibid.

7. Ibid.

Chapter 10 Thoughts for Men

1. M. Esterbrook and Wendy A. Goldberg, "Toddler Development in the Family: Impact of Father Involvement and Parenting Characteristics," *Child Development*, vol. 55 (1984): 740–52; cited in Meg Meeker, *Strong Fathers, Strong Daughters* (Washington, DC: Regency Publishing, 2006), 23.

2. Rebekah Levine Coley, "Children's Socialization Experiences and Functioning in Single-Mother Households," cited in Meeker, *Strong Fathers, Strong Daughters*.

3. *Journal of the American Medical Association* 10 (September 10, 1997), 823–32, and Greg J. Duncan, Martha Hill, and W. Jean Yeung, "Fathers' Activities and Childrens' Attainments," paper presented at a conference on father involvement, October 10–11, Washington, DC, found in Wade F. Horn and Tom Sylvester, *Father Facts* 4th, www.fatherhood.org.; cited in Meeker, *Strong Fathers, Strong Daughters*.

4. Meeker, *Strong Fathers, Strong Daughters*, 24.

5. Lois Mowday, *Daughters without Dads: Offering Understanding and Hope to Women Who Suffer from the Absence of a Loving Father* (Nashville: Oliver-Nelson Books, 1990), 64.

6. Werner Haug and Phillipe Warner, "The Demographic Characteristics of the Linguistic and Religious Groups in Switzerland," *The Demographic Characteristics of National Minorities in Certain European States*, vol. 2 of Population Studies no. 31 (Strasbourg: Council of Europe Directorate General III, Social Cohesion, January 2000); cited in S. Michael Craven, "Fathers: Key to Their Children's Faith," *Christian Post*, June 19, 2011, http://www.christianpost.com/news/fathers-key-to-their-childrens-faith-51331/.

7. Ibid.

8. John Trent and Greg Johnson, *Dad's Everything Book for Sons* (Grand Rapids: Zondervan, 2003), 153.

Conclusion

1. "MTV and the Associated Press Release Landmark Study of Young People and Happiness," MTV, August 20, 2007, http://www.prnewswire .com/news-releases/mtv-and-the-associated-press-release-landmark -study-of-young-people-and-happiness-58300137.html.

Rick Johnson is the bestselling author of *That's My Son*; *That's My Teenage Son*; *That's My Girl*; *Better Dads, Stronger Sons*; and *Becoming Your Spouse's Better Half*. He is the founder of Better Dads and is a sought-after speaker at many large parenting and marriage conferences across the United States and Canada. Rick, his wife, Suzanne, and their grown children live in Oregon. To find out more about Rick Johnson, visit www.betterdads.net.

Encouragement and advice for
moms from family expert

RICK JOHNSON

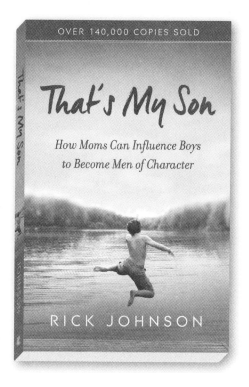

A mother's imprint on her son lasts *forever*.

 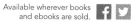

Encouragement and advice for
dads from family expert

RICK JOHNSON

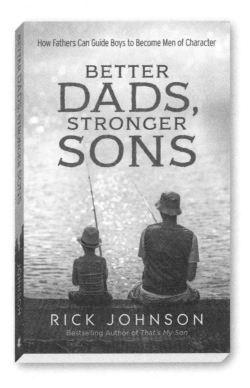

Your son is *counting on you*.

Meet

RICK JOHNSON

at www.BetterDads.net

Connect with Rick on Social Media

 RickJohnsonAuthor

 @betterdads4u